Contents

A Note About the Author

Alexandre Dumas was born in France. He was one of the most popular French writers in the nineteenth century. He wrote books, plays, stories for children and magazine articles.

Dumas was born on 24th July 1802, in Villers-Cotterêts, France. His father was a general in the French army. His mother was the daughter of an innkeeper[1].

In 1822, Dumas went to Paris to work in the house of a rich man, the Duc de Orléans. Dumas became the duke's secretary[2]. In Paris, Dumas met actors and singers, and he began to read as much as possible. He also began to write plays and novels. Dumas wanted to write novels which told the history of France. Many of his stories were about the lives of the Bourbons, the royal family of France.

Dumas loved good food, fine wines and beautiful women. And he liked travelling to different countries. Dumas never had enough money. He spent more money than he earned. He had to write so that he could pay his debts[3].

Dumas fell in love many times. In 1824, he had a love affair[4] with Catherine Lebay and they had a son. The boy was also named Alexandre. He also became a writer.

Dumas married Ida Ferrier in 1842. But their marriage ended a few years later. By 1844, Ida and Dumas no longer loved each other, so they separated. Ida went to live in another home.

Dumas wrote his first, and most successful play, *Mademoiselle de Belle-Isle*, in 1839. He continued to write plays for twenty years. During the 1840s, Dumas wrote a long novel in three parts. These were called *The Three Musketeers* (1844), *Twenty Years After* (1845) and *The Viscount of Bragelonne* (1848–1850). A section of the third story has the title, *The Man in the Iron Mask*. Many movies have been made of this adventure. *The Count of Monte Cristo*, on which this story is based, was printed in a magazine between 1844 and 1845. Each week, another chapter of the story was published.

With the money that he earned from his books, Dumas built a large house, which he named Château de Monte-Cristo. However, by 1850, Dumas had spent all his money and had to sell Château de Monte-Cristo. He immediately wrote another story – *The Black Tulip*. Although this romantic story was very successful, Dumas still had many debts. In 1851, he travelled to Belgium with his friend, the writer Victor Hugo. Dumas was trying to escape from his creditors.

In 1853, Dumas became the publisher of a Parisian newspaper, *Le Mousquetaire* (*The Musketeer*). Five years later, he published a magazine called *Le Monte-Cristo*. He also began a nine-month journey to Russia.

Between 1861 and 1870 Dumas travelled all through Europe. He also had a love affair with an American woman called Adah Menken. But all the travelling, hard work, and worry about money, had made Dumas ill. He died on 5th December 1870 at Puys, near Dieppe, in northern France.

A Note About This Story

A few years before Dumas was born, there were many changes in his country. In 1789 there was a revolution in France. The French people said that they no longer wanted Louis XVI[5] to be their king. They wanted France to be a republic. They wanted to rule[6] the country themselves.

In December 1792, Louis XVI was taken to a court of law. At his trial[7], the people told Louis that he had harmed his country and his people. They said that he was a traitor to France. Louis was accused of treason[8] and executed[9] on 21st January 1793.

At this time, a clever young Corsican named Napoleon Bonaparte was a soldier in the French army. Bonaparte's career[10] was extremely successful. At the age of twenty-seven, Bonaparte was a general. By 1798, he was leading all the French armies in Egypt. His armies won many battles. In 1799, Bonaparte and his supporters[11] began to rule France. In 1804, he was named Emperor of France.

Emperor Napoleon's supporters believed that he had made France a much better, stronger country. Supporters of the royal family, believed that Napoleon only wanted money and power for himself. Napoleon did many good things, but he not allow anyone to speak against him. He controlled the newspapers. And he employed[12] special police agents[13] to work secretly against his enemies.

In 1812, Napoleon led his army into Russia. Thousands of his soldiers died outside the city of Moscow. When Napoleon returned to France, the people no longer supported him. So he abdicated[14].

Napoleon was exiled – he was sent away from France – in April 1814. He went to live on the island of Elba with his advisers and friends. After Napoleon's abdication, Louis XVIII, the brother of Louis XVI, became king. Louis was a member of the Bourbon family. Napoleon escaped from Elba in March 1815. His supporters – the Bonapartists – and the French army welcomed him. Louis XVIII, who was not a popular king, left France. Once again, France was ruled by an emperor.

Emperor Napoleon ruled for only one hundred days. On 18th June 1815, Napoleon's army fought the armies of Prussia, Britain, Holland, Belgium and Germany at Waterloo in Belgium. Napoleon lost the battle and he abdicated again. He was exiled to St Helena, a small island in the Atlantic Ocean. Louis XVIII returned to France and ruled until his death in 1824.

The Places in This Story

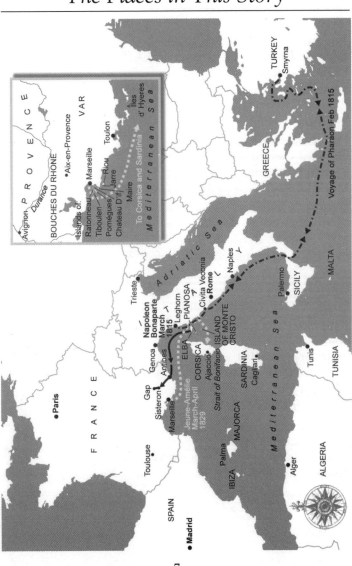

7

The People in This Story

The ship, *Pharaon*
Edmond Dantès – first officer of the *Pharaon*
Leclère – captain of the *Pharaon*
Danglars – cargomaster[15] of the *Pharaon*

Marseille
Mercédès – fiancée of Dantès
Gaspard Caderousse – a tailor
Fernand – cousin of Mercédès
Morrel – the owner of the *Pharaon*
Gérard de Villefort – Prosecutor[16] of Marseille
Marquis de Saint-Méran – a rich politician
Mademoiselle Renée de Saint-Méran – daughter of Marquis
de Saint-Méran, fiancée of Villefort

Paris
Louis XVIII – King of France
Duc de Blacas – King Louis' adviser[17]
Dandré – Minister of Police
Noirtier – Bonapartist

Château d'If
Faria – Prisoner Number 37

The ship, *Jeune-Amélie*
Baldi – captain of the *Jeune-Amélie*
Jacopo – a sailor on the *Jeune-Amélie*

A Picture Dictionary

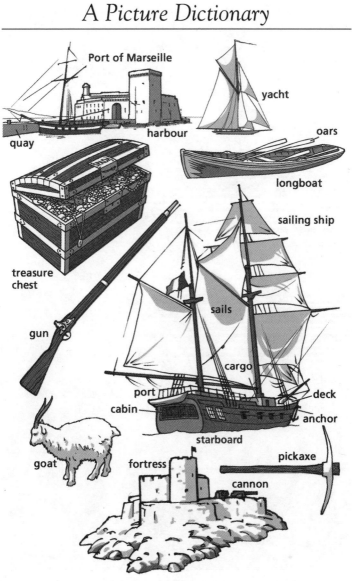

Port of Marseille

quay

harbour

yacht

oars

longboat

treasure chest

sailing ship

gun

sails

cargo

port

cabin

deck

anchor

starboard

goat

fortress

cannon

pickaxe

When he saw Monsieur Morrel, he went to the starboard side of the ship.

1

The Pharaon *Comes Home*

On the 24th February 1815, the ship, *Pharaon*, arrived at the port[18] of Marseille. A large crowd was standing on the quay. The people had come down to the harbour to greet the ship. It was always exciting when a ship arrived in Marseille. And this ship had been built in the city, and the ship's owner lived there. The owner of the *Pharaon* was Monsieur Morrel. He did not wait for his ship to reach the harbour. He immediately jumped into a longboat and rowed[19] towards the *Pharaon*.

A young man was standing on the deck of the *Pharaon*. When he saw Monsieur Morrel, he went to the starboard side of the ship. The young man was the first officer of the *Pharaon*. He was tall, between eighteen and twenty years old, and had thick black hair. His bright, dark eyes were calm and intelligent.

The young man turned round and gave an order to the crew. The sailors ran quickly to their places and waited. Some men stood on the decks. Other men climbed up the tall masts.

'Edmond – Edmond Dantès!' shouted Morrel from the longboat. 'Where is the captain? What's happened to Captain Leclère?'

'Something very sad, sir,' replied the first officer. 'When we were near Civita Vecchia we lost our brave captain.'

'And what has happened to the cargo?' the shipowner asked.

'It's all safe, sir. But poor Captain Leclère —'

'What happened to him?' asked Morrel. 'Did he fall into the sea?'

11

'No, sir, he suddenly became ill and died,' said Dantès. 'He died of brain-fever[20]. We buried him at sea[21].'

'Oh! Poor Captain Leclère! He was only thirty-nine years old,' said Morrel. 'But Edmond, we must all die one day. Did you say that the cargo is safe?'

'Please, come aboard[22], sir,' said Dantès. 'Here is Danglars, the cargomaster. You can ask him about our cargo. He'll also tell you more about the captain's death. I must give some orders to the crew.'

Dantès turned to the sailors on the deck. 'Lower all the sails!' he shouted.

Morrel climbed up the side of the *Pharaon* and greeted Danglars.

'You've heard our sad news, Monsieur Morrel,' said Danglars. The cargomaster was twenty-five or twenty-six years old, and he always had an angry expression[23] on his face. The crew of the *Pharaon* did not like him.

'Yes, poor Captain Leclère,' said Morrel. 'He was a brave and honest[24] man.'

'Yes. And he was an experienced *man* – not a boy,' said Danglars. 'He knew a lot about ships and the sea. He was the kind of captain that you need, sir.'

'But a sailor does not need to be old to understand his work, Danglars,' said Morrel. He watched Dantès give more orders to the crew. 'Look at Edmond. He knows his work well.'

'Yes,' said Danglars. He looked at Dantès and his eyes were full of hate. 'Dantès is young and confident[25]. He began to give orders to the crew before the captain had died! But he also made us lose a day and a half on the voyage. We stopped at the island of Elba.'

'Edmond is the first officer,' said Morrel. 'A first officer has to sail a ship when a captain cannot do his work. But Edmond was wrong to lose time at Elba.'

Morrel called to the young man. 'Edmond! Come here!'

'In a moment, sir,' replied Dantès. He shouted to the men who were standing by the heavy chain which was attached to the anchor. 'Drop the anchor!' he ordered.

Immediately, the sailors let the heavy anchor drop into the sea and the *Pharaon* stopped.

'Do you see?' said Danglars. 'Dantès is like a captain already.'

'He works well,' said Morrel. 'He'll be captain soon.'

This news did not please Danglars. When Dantès came towards Morrel, Danglars moved away.

'You wanted to speak to me, sir?' said Dantès.

'Yes,' said Morrel. 'Why did you stop the ship at Elba?'

'Captain Leclère ordered me to go there,' said Dantès. 'Before he died, he gave me a packet. He told me to take it to Marshall Bertrand on the island.'

Morrel moved closer to Dantès and spoke quietly. 'And did you see Marshall Bertrand?' he asked. 'Did you see Napoleon's adviser?'

'Yes, sir.'

'And did you speak to the emperor?' asked Morrel.

'*He* spoke to *me*,' said Dantès, smiling. 'Emperor Napoleon asked me questions about the *Pharaon*. I told him that the ship belonged to you, sir. Then Napoleon said, "There was a soldier called Policar Morrel in my army at Valence."'

'That's true!' said Morrel, happily. 'Policar Morrel was my uncle. You were right to stop at Elba, Edmond. But don't tell anyone that you spoke with Napoleon. It could bring you trouble.'

'Why?' said Dantès calmly. 'I didn't know what was in the packet. Napoleon only asked simple questions about the ship. He didn't talk about politics. Oh, excuse me, sir! The customs officers[26] are coming aboard.' And Dantès went to the side of the ship.

Danglars came and stood beside Morrel. 'Did Dantès tell you why he delayed the voyage?' he asked.

'He was obeying the last order from Captain Leclère,' replied Morrel.

'And did Dantès give you a letter from the captain?'

'A letter?' said Morrel. 'A letter for me?'

'The captain gave Dantès a letter, as well as the packet for Elba,' said Danglars.

'How do you know about the packet?' asked Morrel.

'I was going past the captain's cabin,' Danglars said. 'The door was open and I saw the captain give the packet and a letter to Dantès.'

'He said nothing to *me* about a letter,' said Morrel. 'But if there *is* a letter, Edmond will give it to me.'

'Perhaps I made a mistake. Please say nothing about it to Dantès,' said Danglars. The cargomaster walked away when Dantès returned to the shipowner.

'Edmond, will you come and have dinner with me this evening?' asked Morrel.

'Excuse me, sir. But I must visit my father tonight,' said the young man.

'Oh, yes,' said Morrel. 'I haven't seen your father for a few weeks, but I think that he's well. You're a good son, Edmond. Visit your father, then come and see me.'

'Please excuse me again,' said Dantès. 'There is another person that I must see.'

'Of course!' said Morrel. 'You'll want to see Mercédès. She visited me three times to ask about news of the *Pharaon*. Edmond, you have a very beautiful lover!'

'Mercédès isn't my lover – she is my fiancée,' said Dantès. 'She's the woman that I'm going to marry.'

'I wish you happiness and a long life,' said Morrel. 'But tell me, did Captain Leclère give you a letter for me before he died?'

14

'No, sir,' said Dantès. 'Captain Leclère couldn't write. Now, I must ask for some time away from my work. After my marriage, I have to go to Paris.'

'Take all the time that you need,' said Morrel. 'The *Pharaon* will not sail for three or four months.' He smiled and put a hand on Dantès' arm. 'And the ship can't sail again without the new captain.'

'Do you mean that *I* shall be the captain of the *Pharaon?*' cried Dantès. 'Oh, thank you, Monsieur Morrel! My father and Mercédès will be very pleased.'

'That's good, Edmond. Take the longboat and go to your father. Visit Mercédès in Les Catalans[27]. And then come to me.'

'Shall I take you ashore, sir?' asked Dantès.

'No, I'll stay aboard and speak to Danglars about the cargo,' said Morrel. 'Were you happy with his work on this voyage?'

'Danglars doesn't like me,' said Dantès quietly. 'We had an argument near the island of Monte Cristo. But I've nothing bad to say about his work. He's a good cargomaster.'

'You're a good man, Edmond,' said Morrel. 'Go now, and good luck to you!'

Morrel watched the young man jump into the longboat. In a few minutes, Dantès had rowed to the quay.

Morrel turned away and saw Danglars standing a few metres away. The cargomaster was staring at Dantès. He had an angry expression on his face.

2

Mercédès

Louis and Edmond Dantès lived in a small, simple house in one of the city's narrow streets. The old man gave a cry of joy when he saw his son.

'My boy!' said Louis. The old man's face was pale and his body began to shake.

'What's wrong?' asked Edmond. 'Are you ill?'

'No, my dear son! I didn't know that the *Pharaon* had arrived in Marseille. This is a wonderful surprise. Tell me all the news of the voyage.'

'First, I have sad news, father,' said Edmond. 'Captain Leclère is dead. I didn't want that to happen, of course. But now Monsieur Morrel tells me that *I'll* be captain of the *Pharaon*! And I'll be paid well. Do you understand, father? I'm going to be a captain and I'm not yet twenty!'

'That is good news,' said the old man in a weak voice. And he sat down in a chair.

'There *is* something wrong,' said Edmond. 'You're ill!'

'I'm not ill,' answered Louis. 'I'm just a little tired.'

'You need a glass of wine,' said Dantès. 'Where do you keep the wine?' He began to look in the cupboards.

'T–there is no wine,' said the old man.

'What! Why is there no wine?' said Edmond. 'Didn't I leave you enough money before the voyage? I gave you two hundred francs before I left three months ago.'

'Yes,' replied his father. 'But I had to pay our debt to Caderousse.'

'But the debt to Caderousse was one hundred and forty francs,' said Edmond. 'Have you lived for three months on only sixty francs?' He took all the money from his pockets

16

and put it on the table. 'Here, take this. I earned it on the voyage. Buy some food and drink immediately.'

Edmond heard footsteps outside the house. 'Who's coming here, now?' he said.

'It's Caderousse,' said the old man. 'He'll be coming to give you his good wishes.'

'Then his lips will say one thing while his head thinks something else,' Edmond said to himself.

Caderousse came to the door. He was holding a piece of cloth in his hands. Caderousse was a tailor[28]. His shop was beside the house where Louis and Edmond Dantès lived.

'Edmond Dantès!' said Caderousse, smiling and showing his white teeth. 'You've returned!'

'Yes, Caderousse,' said Edmond in a polite, cold voice. 'Do you have a problem? Can I help you?'

Caderousse smiled again. 'Thank you,' he said. '*I* don't want any help. But sometimes there are others who need me. Not you, sirs. I gave you money, but you've paid me.'

Caderousse walked round the room. 'I met my friend, Danglars, in the city,' he said. 'He told me that you were in Marseille again, Edmond.' The tailor's eyes shone brightly when he saw the money on the table. 'And you're now a rich man,' he said.

'This money isn't mine, it's my father's,' said Edmond.

'Danglars told me that you're going to be the new captain of the *Pharaon*,' said Caderousse. 'All your friends will be happy when they hear about your good luck. And I know *one* young lady who'll be pleased.'

'Yes, Mercédès,' said Louis. 'Edmond, go and see your fiancée.'

'You were right to come home quickly,' said Caderousse unpleasantly. 'Mercédès is a fine girl, and fine girls have many admirers[29]. Go and see her and give her your good news.'

'I will,' said Edmond. And he left the house.

Caderousse talked to the old man for a minute or two, then he left. He walked to the corner of the Rue Senac, where Danglars was waiting for him.

'Did you see young Dantès?' asked Danglars.

'I did,' said Caderousse, smiling. 'He believes that he will be captain of the *Pharaon*.'

'Dantès is not captain yet,' said Danglars. '*Is* he going to marry the beautiful Mercédès?'

'Yes,' said Caderousse. 'But he could have trouble there. Mercédès has a handsome young admirer. He's a twenty-one-year-old Catalan, and he's her cousin.'

Danglars looked pleased about this. 'Let's go to La Réserve and have a drink while we wait for news,' he said.

———

A hundred metres from La Réserve café, was Les Catalans. Mercédès lived in a small white house in this village. She was a beautiful girl, with shining black hair, large dark eyes and a pretty figure. She was seventeen years old.

Mercédès was talking to a tall young man. He was her cousin, Fernand.

'Mercédès,' said Fernand. 'Please, tell me that you will marry me!' He looked at Mercédès with love in his eyes.

'I've answered you a hundred times, Fernand,' said Mercédès. 'You must be very stupid to ask me again.'

'Don't you want me to be happy?' said Fernand. 'For ten years, I've dreamt that you'll be my wife. I love you, Mercédès!'

'Fernand! I've never done anything to make you love me,' the girl replied. 'And I don't want to marry you. I love you like a brother, that is all.'

'You believe that Dantès will return,' said Fernand. 'That is why you're saying this. But perhaps he doesn't love you now. Or perhaps he's dead!'

'Fernand!' cried Mercédès. 'I love Edmond!'

'And will you always love him, and not me?' Fernand asked, holding Mercédès' hand.

'I'll love him for as long as I live,' said Mercédès.

'But if he's dead?'

'Then I shall die too.'

'But perhaps he's forgotten you and —'

'Mercédès!' called a voice from outside the house.

'Oh!' cried the young girl. Her eyes shone with happiness. 'He's here! He *hasn't* forgotten me!' And she ran to open the door. 'Edmond, I'm here!' she said.

In a moment, Dantès and Mercédès had their arms around each other.

At first the lovers saw nothing around them. But then Dantès saw Fernand.

'Oh,' he said. 'I didn't know that anyone else was here.'

'This is my cousin, Fernand,' said Mercédès. 'He's my friend, and he'll be your friend too, Edmond.'

'Hello, Fernand,' said Dantès, and he politely held out his hand. But Fernand did not shake Edmond's hand. In fact, he did not move. He had an expression of hate on his face.

'I didn't expect to meet an enemy here,' said Dantès, after a moment.'

'An enemy!' said Mercédès. 'There's no enemy here. There's only Fernand, who will shake your hand and greet you like a friend.'

The young woman looked angrily at her cousin. As soon as he had shaken Dantès' hand, Fernand turned and left the house.

———

'Hello, Fernand!' called a voice. 'Where are you going?'

The speaker was the tailor, Caderousse. He was sitting outside La Réserve with Danglars. The two men had been drinking wine for several hours. Caderousse was now very drunk. Fernand looked at them for a few seconds. Then he came to their table and sat with them.

'You look like a disappointed lover, Fernand!' said Caderousse, laughing loudly. He gave the young man a glass of wine. Then he filled his own glass, for the eighth or ninth time.

'You didn't think that Dantès was going to return to Marseille so suddenly, did you?' said Danglars. 'Perhaps you thought that he was dead. Or perhaps you thought that he had found another lover. When is Dantès going to marry the beautiful Mercédès?'

'They haven't chosen a date yet,' said Fernand.

'No, but their wedding will be soon,' said Caderousse. 'Let's drink to the marriage of Captain Edmond Dantès and the beautiful Mercédès!' As he lifted his glass, he spilt wine on his clothes.

Fernand threw his glass of wine onto the ground and Caderousse laughed loudly. Then he saw two young people walking towards the café.

'Ah! Look, Fernand!' he said. 'Two lovers are coming this way. See how they kiss each other's lips and look into each other's eyes. It's Edmond and Mercédès!'

Fernand's face had become red and he looked down at the table.

'Hello, Dantès!' called Caderousse. He lifted his wine glass again. 'Are you too proud to speak to your friends?'

'No, sir,' replied Dantès.

'When is your wedding day?' asked Danglars.

'Tomorrow, or the next day,' said Dantès. 'We'll have the wedding feast here, in La Réserve. Please come and celebrate with us. There will be good food and wine. After the feast, Mercédès and I will go to the priest and he'll marry us.'

'You are marrying quickly, *captain*,' said Danglars.

Dantès smiled. 'I'm not a captain yet,' he said.

'Ah! Look, Fernand!' he said. 'Two lovers are coming this way.'

'But you *are* marrying quickly,' said Danglars.

'I want to get married soon because I must go to Paris after the wedding,' Dantès replied.

'Paris?' said Danglars. 'Do you have business there?'

'Captain Leclère asked me to do something for him,' said Dantès. And he and Mercédès began to walk away.

'I suspect[30] that he's going to deliver Bertrand's letter,' said Danglars to himself. 'And that gives me an idea!'

3

The Letter

Danglars watched Dantès and Mercédès walk away, then he turned to the young Catalan.

'Fernand, do you love Mercédès?' he asked.

'Yes!' said Fernand. 'I love her more than Dantès loves her. I want to kill Dantès. But if he dies, Mercédès will kill herself. She told me this.'

'Perhaps you can stop the wedding. Then Dantès would not have to die,' said Danglars.

He called to a waiter, 'Bring me a pen and some paper!'

A few minutes later, the waiter brought a pen, a pot of ink, and some pieces of paper to the table.

'Dantès stopped at the island of Elba during our voyage,' Danglars told Fernand. 'Perhaps he met Bonaparte there. If someone told the Prosecutor of Marseille that Dantès was a special agent for the Bonapartists, Dantès would be arrested.'

'I'll tell the prosecutor!' cried Fernand.

'No, you mustn't do that,' said Danglars. 'Dantès would suspect that *you* told the prosecutor about his visit to Elba. No, a letter will be perfect.'

The cargomaster smiled and began to write a letter. Danglars usually wrote with his right hand. But now he slowly wrote the letter with his left hand. He was disguising his handwriting.

> THIS LETTER IS FROM A FRIEND OF THE KING. EDMOND DANTÈS, FIRST OFFICER OF THE SHIP, PHARAON, IS GOING TO DELIVER A LETTER TO FRIENDS OF NAPOLEON IN PARIS. YOU WILL FIND PROOF[31] OF THIS CRIME WHEN YOU ARREST HIM. OR YOU WILL FIND PROOF AT HIS FATHER'S HOUSE.

When he had finished writing, Danglars addressed the letter to the Prosecutor of Marseille.

Caderousse had been sleeping for a few minutes. Now he suddenly lifted his head and opened his eyes. He saw the letter that Danglars had written.

'No!' Caderousse cried. 'Dantès is my friend.' The drunken tailor tried to take the letter from Danglars. But he moved too quickly and nearly fell off his chair.

Danglars threw the letter onto the floor in the corner of the café.

'Don't worry about the letter, my friend,' he said to Caderousse. 'It was just a bad joke. You've had too much wine. I'll take you home. Fernand, will you come with us?'

'No,' said Fernand. 'I'm going home.'

When Danglars and Caderousse were twenty metres from the café, Danglars looked back. He smiled. He saw Fernand pick up the letter and walk away quickly.

———

Many guests came to Dantès and Mercédès' wedding feast. Some of them were men from the *Pharaon*. When Morrel came into the café, he told the sailors that Dantès was going to be their new captain. They were pleased.

Mercédès and Edmond were standing with Louis Dantès and Fernand. Danglars and Caderousse went to talk to them.

Caderousse told Edmond that Morrel had arrived at the feast.

'This is the happiest day of my life,' Edmond said, smiling. He looked at Mercédès with love in his eyes. 'It's a quarter past one. At half-past two, my dear Mercédès will become Madame Dantès!'

The guests feasted on the good food and fine wine. They wished good luck to Dantès and Mercédès. Soon it was time for the young people to meet the priest.

'Come with us, everyone!' cried Dantès.

Suddenly, there was a loud knock on the door.

'Open, in the name of the law!' called a voice.

No one spoke and no one moved. The door opened and an officer of police and five soldiers walked in. The soldiers were all carrying guns.

'Why are you here, sir?' Morrel asked the police officer.

The man did not reply. 'Which of you is Edmond Dantès?' he asked.

'I am,' said Edmond. 'What do you want?'

'Edmond Dantès, I'm here to arrest you,' said the officer.

Mercédès cried out and began to weep.

'This must be a mistake!' said Morrel.

'What crime am I accused of?' asked Dantès.

'You'll be told later,' said the officer.

Caderousse whispered to Danglars. 'What does this mean?'

'I don't know,' replied Danglars.

Caderousse looked for Fernand, but he could not see him in the café. 'This is about that letter,' he said to Danglars.

'Don't be stupid,' said the cargomaster.

'But—' began Caderousse.

'Be quiet, you fool!' said Danglars. 'You drank too much wine yesterday. You know nothing about it.'

Dantès was saying goodbye to his friends. 'Don't worry,' he said. 'This is a mistake. I'll return very soon.'

'Edmond Dantès, I'm here to arrest you,' said the officer.

Dantès went down the stairs with the police officer and the soldiers. A carriage was waiting outside La Réserve and he was pushed into it.

Mercédès ran down the stairs to the street. She looked through the window of the carriage.

'Goodbye, my dearest Edmond!' she cried.

'Goodbye, Mercédès,' called Dantès. 'We'll soon meet again.'

Then the horses jumped forward and pulled the carriage down the street. In a few minutes, the carriage had gone around a corner and disappeared.

'Wait for me here, all of you,' said Morrel. 'I'll follow Dantès. The officer will take him to the prosecutor's office, I am sure. I'll go there. I'll bring you news as soon as I can.'

At that moment, Fernand came into the room and sat down. His face was very pale. He had a glass of water in his hand. His hand shook as he drank from the glass.

'This is all Fernand's work, I'm sure,' Caderousse said to Danglars quietly.

'No, he couldn't have done this,' said Danglars. 'He's too stupid.'

Time passed slowly, but at last Morrel returned to the café. He had a worried expression on his face. Mercédès, Louis and all the guests came and stood round him.

'Dantès is in serious trouble,' said Morrel. 'He is accused of treason. Prosecutor Villefort said, "Dantès is a traitor to the king. He is a Bonapartist agent."'

Mercédès cried out, and Louis Dantès sat down on a chair.

Caderousse moved closer to Danglars. 'You lied to me,' he whispered. 'The letter that you wrote yesterday reached the Prosecutor of Marseille! But I can't let an old man and an innocent girl die of unhappiness. I'll tell the prosecutor that Dantès is not guilty.'

'Be silent, you fool!' said Danglars. He held Caderousse's

arm. 'Perhaps Dantès isn't innocent. Who can be sure? The *Pharaon* did stop at Elba, and Dantès did go ashore. Perhaps he has Bonapartist letters or papers with him. The prosecutor will find them. But there is danger for us. Any friend of Dantès, or anyone who works with him, will be suspected of treason too.'

Caderousse thought for a moment. 'We'll wait and see if Dantès is guilty or innocent,' he said.

The guests began to leave the café. Louis Dantès' friends took him back to his house, and Fernand took Mercédès to her home. Very soon, everyone in Marseille had heard the news of Edmond's arrest.

Later that day, Morrel saw Danglars and Caderousse.

'Can you believe that this has happened, Danglars?' Morrel said. 'Dantès … arrested for treason!'

'I was suspicious when Dantès stopped the *Pharaon* at Elba,' said Danglars. 'Remember, I told you this when the ship returned on 24th February.'

'Yes, yes. Did you tell your suspicions to anyone else?' asked Morrel.

'No, I didn't,' said the cargomaster.

'You're a good man, Danglars,' said Morrel. 'And the *Pharaon* has no captain now.'

'The *Pharaon* cannot leave Marseille for three months,' said Danglars. 'We have to make some repairs to *Pharaon*. Then we have to load a cargo onto the ship. Let's hope that Dantès is a free man again after three months. Until then, I can take care of the ship for you.'

'Thank you, Danglars. I'll go and see Prosecutor Villefort, again. I'll ask for news of Dantès. Go to the ship. I'll meet you there later.'

The shipowner walked away and Danglars turned to Caderousse. 'All goes well,' he said to the tailor.

'But your false letter to Villefort —' began Caderousse.

'Fernand must have sent the letter!' said Danglars. 'He's jealous[32] of Dantès. He wants Mercédès for himself. He must have picked up the letter. Did he copy it onto another piece of paper? Or did he send *my* letter? Luckily, I disguised my handwriting! The prosecutor won't know that I betrayed[33] Dantès.'

'But *is* Dantès a traitor – a Bonapartist?' said Caderousse.

'Perhaps. We must say nothing!' said Danglars. 'If there is trouble, then it was Fernand who betrayed Dantès.'

'Yes, yes. You're right. We'll say nothing,' said Caderousse. And he began to feel a little happier.

4

Villefort

In a large house in the centre of Marseille, another wedding feast was taking place. Some of the most important people in Marseille were guests at this celebration. They were talking about Napoleon.

'Bonaparte will never rule France again,' they said. 'He's gone forever. He's exiled to the island of Elba. A king rules our country again.'

An old man stood up and lifted his glass of wine.

'Let's drink to the health of[34] King Louis!' he said.

The man was the Marquis de Saint-Méran and he was a rich and powerful politician.

Other guests lifted their glasses and repeated the old man's words. One of the men who drank to the health of the king was Gérard de Villefort.

Villefort was a very happy man. This was his wedding feast. He was going to be married to Renée Saint-Méran, the daughter of the Marquis Saint-Méran. Although he was only twenty-seven, Villefort had an important position in the city. He was the Prosecutor of Marseille. Villefort smiled happily. He knew that his career would improve after the marriage.

An hour later, Villefort received a message and returned to his office. His friend, the shipowner Morrel, was waiting outside the house.

'Edmond Dantès, the first officer of my ship, has been arrested,' said Morrel.

'I know,' said Villefort. 'I'm going to speak to Dantès now. I was told that he had been brought here.'

'Dantès is an honest man,' said Morrel. 'I'm sure that he's innocent. He isn't a traitor. The charge must be wrong.'

'Don't worry,' said Villefort. 'I'll find out if he is a traitor, or not.'

Villefort went into his house and gave an order to a police officer. A few minutes later, Villefort was sitting in his office. He was looking at the pale, calm face of a young suspect who was standing in front of him.

'Who and what are you?' the prosecutor asked.

'My name is Edmond Dantès,' replied the young man. 'I am the first officer of the *Pharaon*, which is owned by Monsieur Morrel.'

'What is your age?'

'Nineteen.'

'What were you doing when you were arrested?'

'I was at my wedding feast,' answered Dantès. 'I was going to be married.'

Villefort saw Dantès' happiness when he said this. He thought of his own wedding feast. He quickly continued with his questions.

'Were you ever a sailor in Napoleon's navy? Or are you a supporter of Napoleon now?' asked Villefort, coldly.

'No, sir.'

'Do you have strong political opinions[35]?' asked Villefort.

'I don't have *any* political opinions,' replied Dantès. 'I know nothing about politics.'

'Do you have any enemies?' asked Villefort.

'Only powerful, important people have enemies,' Dantès replied. 'And I'm not an important person.'

'And what do the crew of the *Pharaon* think of you?' asked the prosecutor.

'The men who work with me love me like a brother, and they respect[36] me.'

'Is anyone jealous of you?' said Villefort. 'You're only nineteen but you're going to be a captain soon. And you're going to marry a pretty girl who loves you. Perhaps someone is jealous of your good luck.'

Villefort took a letter from his pocket and gave it to Dantès. 'Do you recognize[37] the writing on this letter?'

Dantè's face became pale. He began to be afraid.

'No, I don't recognize this writing,' he said. 'The words look strange. Perhaps the writing is disguised. But the person who wrote this letter must hate me.'

'Now, tell me the truth,' said Villefort. '*Are* you a traitor? Are you an agent for Bonaparte? Is anything in this letter correct?'

'No – er – yes,' said Dantès. 'I'll tell you what happened. The *Pharaon* was taking a cargo from Smyrna[38] to Marseille. We were going to stop at Trieste and Naples. When we left Naples, Captain Leclère became ill. He had brain-fever. He was very ill for several days. There was no doctor on the ship and we could not help the captain. Before he died, Captain

Leclère called me to his cabin. "My dear Dantès," he said. "I have something to ask you. I want you to make me a promise[39]. After my death, take the ship to the island of Elba. Go to the fortress[40] on Elba and find Napoleon's adviser. His name is Marshall Bertrand. Give him this packet. Perhaps he'll give you a letter and some orders. Promise that you will do this." I made the promise and the next day Captain Leclère died.'

'What did you do after he died?' asked Villefort.

'I sailed to Elba and went ashore alone,' said Dantès. 'I

gave the packet to Marshall Bertrand. He gave me a letter for someone in Paris. After my marriage, I was going to take it to Paris.'

'Well, your story *sounds* true,' said Villefort. 'And you were only following the orders of your captain. Give me the letter from Bertrand. You must promise to return here, if I need to see you again.'

'Am I free, sir?'

'Yes,' said Villefort, 'but first give me Bertrand's letter.'

'*You* have it, sir,' said Dantès. 'The police officer took it from me when I was arrested.' He pointed at Villefort's desk. 'The letter is in that packet of documents.'

Dantès turned to leave the room. Villefort looked down at the packet on his desk.

'Wait!' he said. 'What name was on the letter?'

'Monsieur Noirtier, 13 Rue Coq-Héron, Paris,' said Dantès.

Villefort picked up the packet and opened it. There was now an expression of fear on his face.

'Monsieur Noirtier, 13 Rue Coq-Héron,' he said. His face had become very pale and his hand shook as he picked up the letter.

31

'Yes,' said Dantès. 'Do you know the gentleman?'

'What? No!' answered Villefort. 'I'm not a friend of the king's enemy!'

Dantès now began to feel afraid again. 'I don't know what is written in the letter,' he said.

'But you knew that it was addressed to Monsieur Noirtier,' said Villefort. 'Did you show this letter to anyone?'

'No, sir,' said Dantès.

Villefort opened the letter and read it. Then he put his hands over his face.

'What is the matter?' asked Dantès.

Villefort looked at the letter again. 'Does Dantès know what is in this letter?' he thought. 'Does he know that Noirtier is my *father*? And does he know that Noirtier is a supporter of Napoleon? If he does know this, then my career is ruined!'

Villefort tried to speak calmly. 'Dantès,' he said. 'Before I let you go, I must speak with someone. You must stay here a little longer. The only problem for you is this letter, and ...' He stood up, went across to the fireplace, and threw the letter into the flames. ' ... you see? It's gone.'

'Thank you, sir, you're very kind,' said Dantès.

'Say nothing about this to anyone,' said Villefort. 'If anyone asks you about the letter – you know nothing about it.'

Villefort opened the door and called a police officer. He spoke quietly to the officer. Then he turned to Dantès.

'Follow this officer,' he said.

When they had gone, Villefort walked round the room.

'Oh, father!' he cried. 'Your political opinions are going to harm my career and my happiness!'

Then he remembered the words in the letter. 'But perhaps there *is* a way that your politics can help me,' he said.

He sat down at his desk and wrote a letter to the king's adviser in Paris.

5

The Château d'If

Dantès was taken from Villefort's office and locked in a small room. At ten o'clock that evening, four soldiers came to the room. They took him outside to a carriage that was waiting in the street. Dantès looked at the soldiers.

'Where are you taking me?' he asked.

'You'll soon know,' said the officer. 'We can't tell you.'

Then a soldier pushed his gun against the young man's back and they all got into the carriage.

The carriage went quickly through the streets of the city and down to the harbour. A longboat, with four sailors in it, was waiting at the quay. The soldiers put Dantès into the boat, then they got into it too. The sailors picked up the oars and began to row the boat out of the harbour.

'Where are you taking me?' asked Dantès.

'Don't you know?' said the officer. 'Turn round and look.'

Dantès turned. The boat had passed the entrance of the port. On the left, he saw the dark shadow of the island of Ratonneau. And on the right, he saw the black shape of the island of If.

On the top of steep rocks, was a great prison fortress – the Château d'If. The thick stone walls of the prison had stood for three hundred years. Many stories were told about this terrible place.

'The Château d'If!' cried Dantès. 'But – but Monsieur de Villefort promised —'

'I don't know what Monsieur de Villefort promised,' said the officer. 'We have to take you there. Those were our orders. No, stop!'

Dantès had stood up. He tried to jump out of the boat and

On the top of steep rocks, was a great prison fortress – the Château d'If.

into the sea. But two of the soldiers held him and he fell back into the boat. The officer pointed his gun at Dantès.

'If you move again, I'll shoot you,' he said.

Half an hour later, the longboat reached the island of If. The soldiers pulled Dantès out of the boat and held his arms behind his back. Then they pushed him up the wet stone steps and through the gate of the prison.

Dantès looked around. He was in a courtyard[41] which was surrounded by high walls. It was now completely dark. The only light came from a few lamps that were fixed to the walls.

The soldiers and their prisoner waited in the courtyard for ten minutes. Then a voice called, 'Where is the prisoner?'

'Here!' replied the soldiers.

'I'll take him to a cell,' said the voice. It was one of the jailers[42]. 'Let him follow me.'

The soldiers pushed Dantès forward. 'Go!' they said.

The young man followed the jailer to a small room which had stone walls and a thick wooden door.

'You'll stay here tonight,' the jailer said. 'The governor[43] is asleep. Perhaps he'll see you tomorrow. Here is bread, water and a bed. You now have everything that a prisoner can want.'

Before Dantès could answer him, the jailer shut and locked the door and went away. Dantès stood alone in the darkness. For the rest of the night, he did not sleep. He walked round and round the cell.

In the morning, the jailer returned.

'Are you hungry?' he asked.

'I want to see the governor,' said Dantès.

The jailer shook his head and left the cell.

Dantès threw himself onto the floor and wept tears of anger. 'What is my crime? I've done nothing wrong!' he shouted. 'Why am I in this terrible place?'

At the same time the next morning, the jailer returned.

'I want to see the governor,' Dantès said again.

'It's not allowed,' the jailer told him.

'What *is* allowed?'

'If you have money, you can buy better food, and books to read,' said the jailer. 'If you behave well, you can walk outside for a few minutes each day. Perhaps one day you might meet the governor.'

'How long will I have to wait before I see the governor?' asked Dantès.

'A month – six months – a year,' the jailer replied.

'I can't wait that long,' said Dantès. 'I want to see him now.'

'If you wish for impossible things,' said the jailer, 'you'll go mad. There was a prisoner here who tried to buy his freedom. He told us that he would give us a million francs. He was kept in this cell.'

'When did he leave it?' asked Dantès.

'Two years ago.'

'Did the governor let him go free?'

'No. The prisoner went mad. He was put in a dungeon⁴⁴.'

'If you help me, I'll give you three hundred francs,' said Dantès. 'Please go to Marseille, find a young girl called Mercédès, and give her a letter from me.'

'I can't do that,' said the jailer. 'I would lose my job. And I don't want your money. I earn two thousand francs a year.'

'Then one day, I'll hit you when you enter this cell!' said Dantès.

'You *are* going mad,' said the jailer.

He went out and returned with four soldiers. 'Take this prisoner to the dungeon,' he said. 'Put him in cell thirty-four. This man is now Prisoner Number 34.'

———

Villefort was going to Paris to see the king's adviser. Before he left Marseille, a beautiful young girl stopped his carriage in the street. It was Mercédès. She spoke to Villefort through the carriage window.

'Sir, where is Edmond Dantès?' she asked.

'I can't tell you,' said Villefort. 'I don't know. I can do nothing for him. Now, step away from my carriage.'

As Villefort travelled towards Paris, he thought about Dantès. He had sent an honest young man to the terrible Château d'If. He had ended the happiness of an innocent young man and his beautiful fiancée.

6

The King

Louis XVIII, the King of France, was in his favourite room in his palace. Louis was reading a book of poetry. And at the same time, he was listening to some advice from a small, fifty-year-old man.

'Majesty, I'm worried,' said the man. His name was the Duc de Blacas, and he was the king's friend and adviser.

'What are you worried about, Blacas?' asked the king, turning the pages of his book.

'I believe that trouble is coming from the south of the country,' said Blacas. 'Will you send men into the provinces[45] of Languedoc, Provence and Dauphiné? Send honest men that you can trust[46]. Ask them to find out the feelings of the people in these southern provinces. Majesty, I'm afraid that Bonaparte, or some of his supporters, are planning to kill you.'

'Are you trying to frighten me, my friend?' said the king.

'I've received a letter from a man in the south, Majesty,' said Blacas. 'I trust this man. The letter said that there is a plot[47] against you. You are in great danger, Majesty.'

At that moment, Dandré, the Minister of Police, entered the room.

'Come in, Dandré!' cried the king. 'Tell Blacas the latest news about Bonaparte. Blacas is trying to frighten me. He's talking about a plot by the Bonapartists!'

'Monsieur Blacas,' Dandré said to the duke. 'There is good news from Elba. My officers have reported that Bonaparte is very tired. And they say that, very soon, he will be mad.'

'Mad?' said Blacas.

'Yes,' answered Dandré. 'Sometimes Napoleon weeps. Sometimes he laughs like a madman. Two or three older members of his staff wanted to come back to France. Then Napoleon said, "Go and serve[48] the good king." Those were his words.'

'Well, Blacas?' said King Louis. 'What do you think about *this* news?'

'Perhaps I was wrong about Bonaparte's plans,' said Blacas to the king. 'But please speak to the person who sent me the information.'

'Oh, very well,' said Louis. He put down his book and picked up a document from his desk. He turned towards the Minister of Police. 'Now, Dandré, do you have a new report from Elba? I've read this report which has a date of 20th February. Today is 4th March.'

'Majesty, a new report will arrive very soon,' said Dandré. 'Perhaps it's arrived since I left my office.'

'Then go and find out,' said the king. 'I'll wait here.'

'I'll return in ten minutes,' said Dandré. And he left the room quickly.

'I'll go and find my messenger, Majesty,' said Blacas.

'Who *is* your messenger?' asked the king.

'Gérard de Villefort,' said Blacas. 'He's the Prosecutor of Marseille.'

'Villefort!' cried the king. 'Why didn't you tell me his name earlier?'

'Majesty, I didn't think that you would know it,' said Blacas.

'But I do, Blacas,' said the king. 'I know all about Villefort. He's clever and ambitious[49]. He'll be useful to us. And you know his father's name.'

'His father, Majesty?'

'Yes,' replied Louis. 'Villefort's father is called Noirtier.'

'Noirtier ... the *Bonapartist*?' said Blacas. He was surprised. 'Majesty, do you wish to employ the son of a Bonapartist?'

'Villefort wants to improve his career,' said the king. 'He wants more power. He'll sell his own father to get that power. Where is Villefort now?'

'He's outside the palace,' said Blacas. 'He's waiting in my carriage.'

'Bring him to me at once,' said the king.

Blacas returned with Villefort a few minutes later.

'Villefort,' said the king. 'The Duc de Blacas tells me that you have some interesting information for me.'

'Majesty,' said Villefort, bowing[50] towards King Louis. 'I have news of a plot against you. Bonaparte has left Elba and he's going to Italy. He's either going to the city of Naples, or somewhere on the coast of Tuscany. I'm afraid that I do not know which place. But you know that he has friends in Italy and France.'

'Yes,' said Louis. 'Where did you get this information?'

'I got it from a man in Marseille,' replied Villefort. 'My men had been watching him for some time. I suspected that the man was a traitor. My men arrested him and I questioned him. Then I immediately came to Paris.'

'Who is this man?' asked Louis. 'And why do you suspect that he's a traitor?'

'Majesty, the man is a sailor,' replied Villefort. 'He went to the island of Elba and met Marshall Bertrand there. Bertrand gave the sailor a message for a Bonapartist in Paris.'

'What is the name of this Bonapartist?' asked the king.

'The sailor wouldn't tell me the man's name,' said Villefort. 'But the message told the people of Paris that Bonaparte was returning soon. And it promised that Bonaparte would rule France again.'

'And where is this sailor now?'

'He's in prison, Majesty.'

'Do you think that this is a serious plot?' asked the king.

'I do, Majesty,' said Villefort. 'I left my own wedding feast to come here and give you the news.'

'Is it true that you're going to marry the daughter of the Marquis de Saint-Méran?' asked Louis.

'Yes, Majesty,' said Villefort. 'Mademoiselle Renée de Saint-Méran is my fiancée.'

'Very well,' said Louis. 'Now don't worry about this plot, Villefort. My men have been watching the Mediterranean coast for ten months. But thank you for coming to me.'

'Ah, here is Dandré!' said Blacas.

The Minister of Police had come into the room. He was holding a report in his hand and he had a worried expression on his face.

'What's the matter, Dandré?' asked the king.

'Majesty —' began the minister, his voice was shaking.

'Well?' said the king. 'Tell me what has happened!'

'I have a new report,' said Dandré. 'Napoleon left Elba on 26th February. And he came ashore on 1st March.'

'Where did he come ashore?' asked the king, quickly.

'Majesty, he came ashore near the town of Antibes,' said Dandré.

'He came ashore on 1st March? And you only heard the news *today*? Today is 4th March!' The king was angry now.

'Majesty, it's true,' said the Minister of Police, unhappily.

'Napoleon is in France!' said Louis, shaking his head.

'Majesty,' said Villefort. 'The people of the southern provinces hate Napoleon. If he's there, it'll be easy to get the people of Languedoc and Provence to fight against him.'

'Yes, that *is* true,' said Dandré. 'But Napoleon has quickly travelled north. He's moved through the towns of Gap and Sisteron – in the eastern part of Dauphiné province.'

'Is he coming to Paris?' asked the king. Dandré did not answer. The king turned towards Villefort.

'What about the province of Dauphiné?' he asked. 'Will the people of Dauphiné fight against Napoleon? Will they support me?'

'No, Majesty,' said Villefort sadly. 'They're Bonapartists.'

'Dandré, how many men are with Napoleon?' asked the king.

'I don't know,' answered Dandré.

'Dandré!' the king shouted. 'You have an office, a police department and fifteen hundred francs to pay special agents. You have these things so that you can find out what is

41

happening in France. But you don't know what is happening in *one* area – the southern coast. Then a prosecutor from a city in the south comes to *me* with information! He has learnt more than you and all your police officers!'

Dandré looked at Villefort with an expression of hate.

'I trust *you*, Blacas,' said the king, turning to his adviser. 'You told me of your suspicions. And you brought Villefort to me when others might have sent him away.'

'Majesty, we can be sure of your army,' said Blacas. 'All your soldiers support you. All reports say —'

'Reports!' said the king. 'How can we know that any reports are correct? But I remember something that may be important! You told me that General Quesnel died here in Paris – in the Rue Saint-Jacques. What have you found out about his death?'

'The Rue Saint-Jacques!' cried Villefort suddenly. 'Oh, I'm sorry, Majesty. But ... '

'Go on,' the king said to Villefort.

'Majesty!' said Dandré quickly. 'I have news about General Quesnel. He didn't kill himself. He was murdered. He disappeared one evening, after he left a Bonapartist club. He was going to meet someone in the Rue Saint-Jacques. A stranger had called at his house that morning. One of Quesnel's servants heard the stranger say the name of the street, but not the number of the house. And we don't know the name of this stranger.'

When Dandré told the king this, Villefort's face went pale. The king turned to him.

'Villefort,' he said. 'Quesnel was not one of Napoleon's agents. He worked for *me*. He was loyal[51] to me. He was trying to find information about Napoleon. But I believe that his murderer was one of Napoleon's supporters.'

'M–Majesty, do we know any more about the stranger who went to Quesnel's house?' asked Villefort.

Dandré answered the question. 'Quesnel's servant said that the stranger was about fifty years old. The man had black hair and thick, black side-whiskers[52]. He wore a blue coat and a hat with a broad brim. Yesterday, one of my agents followed a man who looked like this. But they lost the man between the Rue de la Jussienne and the Rue Coq-Héron.'

As he listened to Dandré, Villefort felt ill. His legs became weak. He thought that he was going to fall to the ground.

'Continue to look for this man, Dandré,' ordered the king.

Then he turned to Villefort. 'You must be tired after your journey,' he said. 'Go and rest. Did you stop at your father's house before you came here?'

'N–no, Majesty,' replied Villefort. 'As soon as I arrived in Paris, I went to Monsieur de Blacas' house.'

'Ah, I forgot,' said the king. He smiled but he also looked carefully at the prosecutor. 'You and your father are not good friends. He's a Bonapartist and you are loyal to me. I thank you for your loyalty. Take this.' Then Louis took a medal[53] from his own coat and gave it to Villefort.

'Majesty!' said Villefort. 'This is an officer's medal! Only army officers who have served bravely receive these medals.'

'Take it,' said Louis again. 'If you cannot serve me here in Paris, you may be able to serve me better in Marseille.'

7

Monsieur Noirtier

Villefort returned to the hotel where he was staying. He called a servant and gave some orders. First, he asked for some breakfast. Then he asked for his carriage to be ready in two hours. He was eating his breakfast when the servant came into the room again. The servant told Villefort that someone had come to see him.

'Who is it?' asked Villefort.

'I don't know,' replied the servant. 'The gentleman won't tell me his name. But he wants to speak to you.'

'What does this person look like?'

'He's about fifty. He has black hair and black side-whiskers. He's wearing a blue coat and a hat with a broad brim.'

'It's him!' thought Villefort.

At that moment, the man came into the room.

'Father!' said Villefort. He turned to the servant. 'Go!' he said.

Noirtier waited until the servant was out of the room. Then he turned to his son. 'Gérard, you aren't very pleased to see me,' he said.

'Father,' said Villefort. 'I am pleased to see you. But I'm a little surprised. I came to Paris to save you.'

'You came to save *me*?' said Noirtier. 'Tell me why.'

'Have you heard of the Bonapartist club in the Rue Saint-Jacques?' asked Villefort.

'Yes,' replied Noirtier, 'the club is in a house at number fifty-three.'

'General Quesnel went there recently,' said Villefort. 'He left his house at nine o'clock in the evening, and his body was found in the River Seine the next day. He had been murdered. You're in danger, father. The king's agents are looking for supporters of Bonaparte.'

'And who told you this story? asked Noirtier.

'The king,' replied Villefort.

'Then I'll tell you another story,' said Noirtier.

'I think that I know it already,' said Villefort. 'Is it the news about Napoleon? I knew it before you did. Three days ago, I knew that Bonaparte was returning to France. I left Marseille immediately and came to Paris.'

'How did you know about this three days ago?' said Noirtier. 'Three days ago, Napoleon hadn't come ashore.'

'I read a letter that had come from Elba. It was addressed to you. I found it in the pocket of Bonaparte's messenger. Father, if anyone else had found it, you would be dead now. You would have been executed.'

Noirtier laughed. 'Executed? I don't believe that! Where is this letter now?'

'I burned it,' said Villefort. 'It was a dangerous letter.'

'It was dangerous for both of us,' said Noirtier. 'But I fear nothing while you are taking care of me.'

'I've done *more* than take care of you, father,' replied Villefort. 'I've saved your life. General Quesnel was a special agent for the king. Quesnel's death was not an accident. He was murdered. The king himself said that the general was murdered.'

45

'The king!' said Noirtier. 'Doesn't Louis know that there are no murders in politics? In politics there are no *men*, there are only *ideas*. In politics, we don't kill a man. We remove something that is in our way. We thought that Quesnel was a loyal Bonapartist. We invited him to the club and told him our plans. When he'd heard and understood everything, he told us that he was loyal to the king! He promised to say nothing about what he had heard. But we didn't believe him. We let him go free, but he didn't return home. What does that mean? Quesnel had an accident, that's all.'

'Be careful, father,' said Villefort. 'Napoleon's return is important for your plans. But Napoleon will not get far. He'll be followed and caught like a wild animal.'

'Oh, no, my son,' said Noirtier. 'Napoleon is on his way to Grenoble at this moment. On 10th or 12th March, he will be at Lyons. And on 20th or 25th March, he will be here, in Paris.'

'He has only a few men with him,' said Villefort. 'The army will stop him.'

'The army is loyal to Napoleon,' said Noirtier. 'The army will bring him to Paris. The people of Grenoble will be happy to give their town to him. Everyone in Lyons will welcome our emperor. Gérard, I knew that you had arrived in Paris half an hour after you came into the city. You told nobody where you were staying, but I found you.'

'The king's agents may be stupid,' said Villefort. 'But they know what you look like. They know that a man with black hair, black whiskers and a blue coat went to Quesnel's house. And they may catch the man with the blue coat soon.'

'Then that man must make a few changes,' said Noirtier. He pulled off his blue coat and went to a table in the corner of the room. He took his son's razor[54] from the table and shaved off his whiskers. Then he cut his hair. He picked up his son's brown coat and put it on.

'Do you think that the police will recognize me now?'

'No, father.'

'Will you see the king again, Gérard?' asked Noirtier.

'Perhaps,' said Villefort.

'Then give Louis this message. "You're wrong about the people of France. Bonaparte is coming. He'll be welcomed. The people want Napoleon to be their emperor again. Go now, and leave France to its real master. He will not hurt you." Tell King Louis this, Gérard. Or, tell him nothing. Tell *no one* why you've come to Paris. Return quickly to Marseille. Goodbye, my son.'

Noirtier left the room. Villefort went to the window and watched his father disappear round the corner of the street. Then he burned his father's coat and hat. An hour later, Villefort began his journey home to Marseille.

8

The Hundred Days

Noirtier's words were true. Napoleon returned to Paris on 20th March and the people of France welcomed him. King Louis XVIII tried to stop this happening, but he had to leave his country. And so Napoleon became Emperor of France – for one hundred days.

Although Villefort had been loyal to the king, Noirtier told Napoleon good things about his son. Villefort kept his position in Marseille, but he could not marry Renée de Saint-Méran. While Napoleon was Emperor, Villefort needed Bonapartist friends to help him. The family of Saint-Méran were loyal supporters of Louis XVIII. But if Louis returned in the future, then Villefort would need Marquis de Saint-

Méran again. If this happened, Villefort would marry Renée de Saint-Méran. The marriage would improve his career.

One morning, Morrel the shipowner, came to see Villefort.

'Sir,' said Morrel. 'You remember that I visited you six weeks ago – before Emperor Napoleon returned to France. I spoke to you about a young man who was the first officer on my ship, the *Pharaon*. His name was Edmond Dantès. Dantès was arrested because he carried a letter from Napoleon on Elba. In February, that was a crime. But it would *not* be a crime today. At that time, you served the king, and couldn't help Dantès. Today you serve Napoleon. So I'm here to ask you this: What has happened to Edmond Dantès?'

'Dantès,' said Villefort, slowly. 'Edmond Dantès.' He opened a large book and turned the pages. At last he looked up at Morrel. 'Are you sure that you have the right name, sir?'

'Yes,' said Morrel. 'I've known Dantès for ten years. Don't you remember? I asked you to help him. You spoke to me coldly. You said, "I'll find out if he is a traitor, or not." You were a loyal supporter of the king! You didn't want to help Bonapartists at that time.'

'Sir,' said Villefort. 'I *did* support King Louis then. I believed that the people wanted him to rule France. When Napoleon returned, I saw how his people loved him and hated Louis XVIII. I believe that the true king is the person who is loved by his people.'

'That's right!' said Morrel. 'And so Edmond —'

'Wait!' said Villefort, turning the pages of his book. 'Here is his name – Dantès – a sailor who was going to marry a young Catalan girl. I remember now. Dantès was accused of treason – a serious crime. I made my report to Paris. He was taken away a week later.'

'Where has he gone?' asked Morrel.

'Oh, he was taken to Fenestrelle prison, on the Sainte

48

Marguerite islands. He'll return one day.'

'But why isn't he here now?' asked Morrel. 'Napoleon's officials should let him go free.'

'You must write to the Minister of Prisons,' said Villefort.

'But the minister receives hundreds of letters every day,' said Morrel. 'He only answers three or four.'

'That is true,' said Villefort. 'But he'll answer a letter that is signed by you *and me*. I'll deliver it.'

Villefort signed Morrel's letter. Then he said, 'I'll send this for you.'

But Villefort did not send the letter to Paris – he kept it. He hoped that one day, Louis would be king again.

Twice during the One Hundred Days, Morrel came to ask about Dantès. And twice, Villefort promised that he would help Dantès and then he sent Morrel away.

On 18th June, 1815, after one hundred days had passed, Louis became king again. Morrel did not visit Villefort again. Soon after Louis returned to France, Villefort married Renée Saint-Méran and they went to live in Toulouse.

Three months after Edmond's arrest, Old Louis Dantès became ill and died. Danglars went to Madrid. He did not want to be a sailor any more. Fernand and Caderousse became soldiers in the army. Mercédès walked through the streets of Les Catalans and wept. She did not want to live without Dantès. She often stood and looked at the sea. Sometimes she thought about killing herself. She thought about jumping into the sea. But she did not.

Edmond Dantès remained in his dungeon at the Château d'If.

9

The Tunnel[55]

It was now 1816. A year had passed since Louis XVIII had returned to Paris. An inspector of prisons[56] came to visit the Château d'If. He met the prison's governor and then went to speak with several prisoners. Each prisoner said that the food was terrible and that they wanted to be free.

'Prisoners always say the same things,' the inspector told the governor. 'They all say, "I'm innocent. I want to be free." Are there any other prisoners to visit?'

'Only the dangerous and mad prisoners,' replied the governor. 'They are in the dungeons.'

The governor, the inspector and two soldiers went down the dark stairs to the dungeons. The cells were cold, wet and dirty. They smelled terrible. The men stopped in front of a small wooden door with the number thirty-four written on it.

'Who's in here?' said the inspector, holding his hand over his nose.

'Prisoner Number 34 – a very dangerous man,' said the governor. 'When he arrived, he tried to kill the jailer.'

'That's true,' said the jailer.

'He must be mad!' said the inspector.

'He'll be mad in another year,' said the jailer. 'He's almost mad now.'

'There's another cell, about twenty metres away,' said the governor. 'The prisoner in *that* cell is a mad priest. He's been here since 1811. He went mad in 1813.'

'I'll speak to both of them,' said the inspector.

Dantès was sitting on the floor in the corner of his cell. The only furniture was a small bed, a chair and a wooden table. On the table there was a jug of water and a plate.

The young man's face was very pale and he had a thick black beard on his face. Dantès only saw daylight for a few hours each day. The light came through a very small window, which was high in one wall. He jumped up to meet the inspector, but the soldiers pushed him away.

'What do you want?' the inspector asked Dantès.

Dantès tried to speak calmly. 'I don't want them to think that I'm mad or dangerous,' he thought.

'Sir, why am I here?' he asked. 'What is my crime? I want a fair trial in a court.'

'When were you arrested, Prisoner Number 34?' asked the inspector.

'The 28th February, 1815 – at 2.30 in the afternoon,' said Dantès.

'Today is the 30th July, 1816,' said the inspector. 'You've only been here for seventeen months.' He turned towards the governor and said, 'You must show me this prisoner's papers.'

'Sir,' said Dantès. 'I know that you can't free me. But please help me to get a fair trial. Please, give me some hope.'

'I can't give you hope,' said the inspector. 'I can only find out about your arrest. Who arrested you?'

'The Prosecutor of Marseille – Monsieur Villefort.'

'Villefort left Marseille,' said the inspector. 'He now lives in Toulouse. Did he have any reason to be your enemy?'

'No, he was very kind to me,' said Dantès.

'Then can I believe what he writes about you?' asked the inspector.

'Yes, sir,' said Dantès.

Later, the inspector looked at Dantès' papers. He also read Villefort's report about Prisoner Number 34:

EDMOND DANTÈS: A dangerous Bonapartist. He helped Napoleon to return from the island of Elba. Put him in a cell alone. Watch him very carefully.

After he had read this, the inspector wrote the words:

Do nothing.

Weeks, months and years passed. Dantès was now twenty-five years old. He was very thin and very dirty. His clothes were torn and his hair and beard were long. He had hoped and prayed to be free. But this did not happen.

One day he looked at his supper. There were a few pieces of bad meat and the small piece of dry bread on his plate. He was already extremely hungry. But he did not eat.

'From today,' he said. 'I'll throw my food out of the window. If I don't eat, I'll die. Then my terrible life here will end.'

But one evening, Dantès heard a noise in the wall of his cell. KNOCK. KNOCK. KNOCK. He heard the knocking sound for nearly three hours, then it stopped. What had made this sound? Several hours later, the knocking began again. It was nearer now. Suddenly the jailer came into the cell and gave Dantès his breakfast. Dantès quickly began to talk. He spoke louder and louder. He was afraid that the jailer would hear the knocking in the wall. But after a minute, the jailer left. He thought that Dantès was mad. The noise continued and it became louder.

'It's another prisoner,' thought Dantès. 'Is he trying to make a tunnel so that he can escape? Or is someone working in the next cell?'

He picked up his plate and knocked it against the wall. Immediately, the sound in the wall stopped. Dantès waited.

'If the knocking starts again, it will be a workman,' he thought. 'But if a prisoner is making the noise, my knock will frighten him. He'll wait until everyone is asleep before he hits the wall of his cell again.'

There was silence. The noise did not begin again.

Three days later, Dantès heard sounds again. Was someone digging a tunnel? He had to help! Dantès looked at the stones in the wall of his cell. If he dug out the cement[57] which was around the stones, he could remove them. But he needed tools. What could he use? Then he had an idea.

He picked up his water jug from the table and dropped it on the stone floor. The jug broke into several pieces. Dantès took two or three of the sharpest pieces and hid them in his bed. When the jailer came again, Dantès spoke to him.

'I dropped the water jug when I was drinking.'

The jailer was angry. 'Be more careful,' he said. He brought Dantès another jug, but he did not take away the broken pieces.

After the jailer left, Dantès began to work on the wall. A broken piece of the jug was a good tool. He began to work on the wall behind his bed. Near the floor of the cell, the cement between the stones was old and soft. Dantès could dig out the cement easily. After many hours, Dantès had dug out the cement from a few of the smaller stones. These stones were now loose. Soon he would be able to pull them out of the wall.

Dantès worked for three days. But then he came to a very large stone that would not move. He could not move it with his fingers, and the sharp pieces of the jug had broken. He needed another tool. Dantès sat and thought. At last, he had an idea. The jailer always brought food in a metal pot and put some of it onto Dantès' plate. That evening, Dantès put his plate on the floor close to the door. When the jailer came into the cell, he stepped on the plate and broke it. Now Dantès could not have any food.

'Please, will you leave the pot?' said Dantès. 'You can take it away when you bring my breakfast.'

'All right,' said the jailer. He did not want to come back with another plate.

Dantès ate his food. Then he used the handle of the pot to dig out the cement around the large stone. After an hour, the stone came out of the wall. Now there was a large hole behind Dantès' bed. Hour after hour, Dantès continued his work. He was digging further into the thick wall. He was slowly making a tunnel. He worked until early the next morning. Before the jailer brought his breakfast, Dantès put the stone back into the wall and put his bed in front of it.

'Did you bring me another plate?' Dantès asked the jailer.

'No,' the jailer replied. 'You break everything. You can keep the pot. I'll put your food into it.'

Dantès said a prayer, and thanked God for his good luck. Now he could use the handle of the pot to dig his tunnel.

When the jailer had gone, Dantès began to work on his tunnel again. He worked all day. Soon the hole was big enough for a man to climb inside it. Dantès listened for sounds from the next cell. But there was silence. Perhaps the prisoner in the next cell did not trust him.

After he ate his supper, Dantès worked for two or three hours. Suddenly he came to a thick piece of wood.

'Dear God!' cried Dantès. 'Don't let me die here! Must I lose all hope?'

'Who talks of God and losing hope at the same time?' said a voice. It seemed to come from under the ground.

'An unhappy prisoner,' replied Dantès.

'What is your name?' said the voice.

'Edmond Dantès.'

'How long have you been here, Edmond Dantès?'

'Since the 28th February, 1815,' said Dantès.

'What was your crime?'

'I did something which helped Napoleon to return to France,' said Dantès. 'I carried a message from him when he was exiled to the island of Elba in 1814.'

'He was exiled?' said the man's voice.

'Yes,' replied Dantès. 'Didn't you know?'

'I've been here since 1811,' said the prisoner. 'Where

have you been digging, Dantès? Where is your tunnel?'

'It's near the floor of my cell,' replied Dantès.

'How do you hide the hole in the wall of your cell?'

'I put a large stone in the entrance of the hole. Then I put my bed in front of it,' said Dantès.

'What's outside the door of your cell?' asked the prisoner.

'A passage which leads to a courtyard,' Dantès said.

'Oh!' cried the prisoner.

'What's wrong?' asked Dantès.

'I – I've dug my tunnel in the wrong direction!' said the prisoner. 'I've made a mistake of nearly five metres. I thought that your wall was the outside wall of the prison.'

'But then the end of your tunnel would have been above the sea,' said Dantès.

'I was going to jump into the sea and swim to one of the islands near here,' replied the prisoner

'Can you swim as far as the islands?' asked Dantés.

'God will give me the strength,' the prisoner replied.

'Who are you?' asked Dantès.

'I'm Prisoner Number 27,' said the voice. 'How old are you?'

'I was nineteen when I was arrested. I'm almost twenty-six now.'

'We'll talk again soon,' said Number 27. 'Wait until I call you.'

Dantès climbed back along his tunnel and into his cell. He was a happy man. He was not alone, he had a friend!

Next morning, Dantès heard three knocks on the wall. He quickly moved his bed and went down onto his knees. He put his head down near the floor of the cell.

'Is that you, Number 27?' Dantès said. 'I'm here.'

'Has your jailer brought your breakfast this morning?' asked the prisoner.

'Yes,' said Dantès. 'He won't return until this evening.'

'Then I can work,' said Number 27.

After about an hour, part of the floor under Dantès fell away. He moved back quickly when small stones and earth disappeared into the hole. Then the head, shoulders, arms and body of a man appeared in the floor of Dantès' cell.

10

Faria

The man who climbed up into Dantès' cell was small and old. He had long grey hair, a thin face and a long, brown and grey beard. He thanked Dantès for his welcome. Then he looked at the hole behind Dantès' bed.

'You removed the stones,' he said. 'But you didn't have the right tools to help you.'

'No,' said Dantès. He was surprised. 'What tools do you have?'

'I took pieces of metal from my bed and made many tools,' said the old man. 'I dug fifteen or sixteen metres to get here. I thought that I was going to the outside wall of the prison. I was going to jump into the sea.'

'Who are you?' asked Dantès. 'What is your name?'

'I'm a priest,' said the old man. 'My name is Faria. I came to the Château d'If in 1811. Before that, I was in the fortress of Fenestrelle for three years.'

'Why are you here, sir?'

'In 1807,' said Faria, 'I spoke against the governments who ruled the regions of Italy. I thought that one king should rule *all* of Italy. But powerful men heard about my political opinions and I was put in prison. My plans failed[58]. And now my tunnel hasn't been successful.'

*Then the head, shoulders, arms and body of a man appeared in
the floor of Dantès' cell.*

Then Faria began to talk about some of the prisoners who had escaped from French prisons.

'Only a few prisoners escaped,' he told Dantès. 'Some men planned for many months to escape. Others waited for a lucky chance[59], and then used it. Let's wait for *our* lucky chance, Dantès. Now, come and see my cell.'

Dantès followed Faria through the tunnel. In one corner of the priest's cell there was an old fireplace. Faria lifted a stone which was in front of the fireplace. Some metal and wooden tools were hidden in this secret place. There were also several books. The pages of each book were covered with hundreds of lines of tiny words.

'I had five thousand books in my library in Rome,' Faria told Dantès. 'Now I spend many hours remembering those books. And I write about my thoughts, and about my life. I write them in *these* books.'

The old man looked down at the tiny words in the pages of the small books.

'But how did you write down your thoughts?' asked Dantès. 'We're prisoners. We're not allowed to have pens, ink and paper.'

'Sometimes they give us fish for our supper,' said Faria. 'I keep the bones of the fish and I make pens from them. And I make paper from pieces of my shirts. I take black soot from the old fireplace and some wine that the jailer brings me. I mix them together and make ink.'

'You're a very clever man, Faria,' said Dantès.

'Now, please tell me your story,' said the old man.

Dantès told Faria everything that had happened on the ship, *Pharaon*. And he told him about his wedding day.

'Only one man in the crew didn't like me,' he said. 'His name was Danglars. He was the cargomaster on the *Pharaon*.'

'Was anyone with you during your last conversation with Captain Leclère?' asked Faria.

'No, we were alone in the captain's cabin,' said Dantès. 'But wait! I remember now! When Captain Leclère gave me the packet for Marshall Bertrand, Danglars went past the cabin door!'

'Did you take anybody with you to the island of Elba?'

'Nobody,' said Dantès.

'Bertrand took the packet and then he gave you a letter,' said Faria. 'Is that right?'

'Yes,' said Dantès. 'I had the letter in my hand when I returned to the *Pharaon*.'

'So Danglars probably saw the letter,' said Faria.

'Yes. That's true,' Dantès replied.

'You were arrested because of another letter,' said Faria. 'Do you remember what it said?'

'I remember every word,' said Dantès. 'The prosecutor showed it to me. It said: "This letter is from a friend of the king. Edmond Dantès, the first officer of the ship *Pharaon*, is going to deliver a letter to friends of Napoleon in Paris. You will find proof of this crime when you arrest Dantès. Or, proof can be found at his father's house." '

'Describe Danglars' handwriting,' said Faria.

'Danglars made strong marks and he wrote quickly. He used a lot of ink,' said Dantès. 'But ... but the handwriting in the letter from Elba was weak. The words were badly written.'

'The writer of the letter disguised his writing!' said Faria.

'And you think Danglars wrote the letter?' asked Dantés.

'Yes, I do,' answered Faria. 'Did anyone want to stop your marriage to Mercédès?'

'There was a young Catalan who loved her,' replied Dantès. 'His name was Fernand.'

'Did Danglars know Fernand?'

'Yes! I saw them together at the café called La Réserve,' said Dantès. 'They were in the café on the evening before my wedding. There was a third person with them – a man named

Caderousse. And wait! I remember now! There was a pen and some paper on the table in the café. I was arrested because of a false letter. Did Caderousse, Danglars and Fernand know about it? I think that they did. But why was I sent to prison without a trial?'

'That question is more difficult to answer,' said Faria. He thought for a moment or two. 'Did you tell the Prosecutor of Marseille your whole story?'

'Yes, I did,' said Dantès. 'He read the letter from Elba and he was very upset about my bad luck.'

'Your bad luck?' said Faria.

'Yes,' replied Dantès. 'The prosecutor burned the letter. He said that he wanted to help me. The letter was the only proof against me. That is what he said.'

'What name and address was on the letter?'

'Monsieur Noirtier, 13 Rue Coq-Héron, Paris.'

'Noirtier,' said Faria. 'I knew a person with that name. What was the prosecutor's name?'

'Villefort,' said Dantès.

Faria laughed loudly. 'Did Prosecutor Villefort tell you never to speak the name Noirtier again?'

'Yes, he made me promise.'

'That's because Noirtier was his father!' said Faria. 'The prosecutor's real name was Noirtier de Villefort. Danglars, Caderousse, Fernand – and then Villefort – they *all* betrayed you.'

Dantès went back through the tunnel to his own cell. He sat and thought about his life. He did not want to kill himself now. He wanted to live. He wanted to escape and take revenge[60] on his enemies.

Faria promised that he would teach Dantès everything that he knew. And Dantès promised to help the old man to dig a new tunnel.

———

Two years passed. Dantès learned many things from Faria. The old priest taught the young man Spanish, English, German and Italian. They talked about philosophy, science, mathematics, poetry and politics. They also began to dig a new tunnel. But the work ended suddenly when Faria became ill.

'I know what is wrong,' said Faria. 'I have brain-fever. I've had the illness before. There's medicine in a small bottle under my bed. When I stop moving and I'm cold like a dead man, open my mouth. Then you must pour eight or ten drops of the medicine into …'

The old man could not finish his sentence. His body began to shake. His face became red and he cried out. He moved his arms and legs about wildly. Faria moved and cried out for two hours, then he became still and cold.

Dantès opened the old man's mouth and poured ten drops of the medicine into it. Then he waited.

The cell became dark. Night fell. At last, Faria sat up. He could not speak, but he pointed to the door and his plate. Dantès understood. He must leave Faria's cell immediately. The jailer was coming with their food.

Dantès crawled back along the tunnel to his own cell. As soon as the jailer left the food, Dantès went back through the tunnel to Faria. The old man was able to speak now.

'I'll never leave Château d'If, Edmond,' he said. 'I can't walk, and I won't be able to swim.'

'We can wait until you're strong again,' said Dantès.

'My dear friend,' said Faria. 'You're young and strong. Don't wait for me.'

'I won't leave you while you are alive,' said Dantès.

The next morning, Faria was a little better. When the priest saw Dantès, he gave him a piece of half-burned paper with writing on it.

'This paper tells where my treasure is hidden,' he said.

'From this day, one half of the treasure belongs to you.'

'Your treasure?' said Dantès.

'Yes. I'll tell you about it,' said the old man. 'I was once a secretary and I lived in Rome. My employer was Cardinal Spada. He was a priest and he was the last member of an old Roman family. The cardinal was not a rich man himself, but his family *were* once rich. In the fifteenth century, the Spadas had to hide their riches because of a cruel and ambitious man called Cesare Borgia. Borgia and his father, Pope Alexander VI, were the most powerful men in Rome. And they wanted to control all of Italy. Borgia murdered people so that he could take their money and property. Borgia knew that the Spada family were rich. So he invited the head of the family, Count Cesare Spada, to dinner. Count Spada knew that Borgia was going to kill him. A few months before, Borgia had murdered two cardinals so that he could have their money and property.

'Before Count Spada went to Borgia's house,' said Faria, 'he wrote a letter to his nephew, Guido. The letter told Guido where the Spadas' riches were hidden. But when he arrived at Borgia's palace, Count Spada saw his nephew talking with Borgia. Guido was also a guest at the dinner. Borgia gave Guido and Count Spada food and wine that contained poison. Both men died that evening.'

'What happened to the letter and the money?' asked Dantès.

'No one ever found the letter or the Spadas' riches,' said Faria. 'Borgia took all of the family's papers and properties. He searched for many months, but he never found the letter and the treasure.

'Years passed,' Faria went on. 'Some Spadas became soldiers, others became bankers or priests. Some Spadas had money, but most of them were poor. The last member of the family – Cardinal Spada – was my employer. *He* also looked for the Spadas' treasure. He searched almost until the day that he died. But he never found it. When he died, all of his papers and some money came to me.

'On 25th December, 1807, two weeks after the Cardinal's death, I was reading the papers for the thousandth time,' said Faria. 'I fell asleep. When I woke it was dark. I took a candle in one hand and found an old piece of paper. I wanted to light the candle, so I put the paper into the fire. I was going to carry a flame to the candle. Suddenly, I saw writing on the paper! The words were written in special ink, and the heat from the fire had made the words appear! I quickly pulled the paper out of the fire, but some of it was burned. It's the paper that you hold in your hand, Edmond.'

'But half the words on each line are missing,' said Dantès.

Faria smiled, then he gave Dantès another piece of paper with writing on it. 'These, I believe, are the missing words,' he said. 'Put the two pieces together and read it.'

Dantès held the two pieces together and read these words:

Today, Cesare Borgia invited me to dinner. I know that Borgia poisoned Cardinal Capra and Cardinal Bentivoglio and took their money and property. Now Borgia wants my property, money and jewels too. But he will not get my treasure. I have hidden it in a secret place. After my death, I want my nephew, Guido Spada, to have all my money, gold and jewels. The treasure is hidden on the island of Monte Cristo. Guido knows the hiding place. Go ashore where there is a little creek. Walk east until you see a line of rocks. Lift the twentieth rock and find the entrance of two caves. The treasure is in the corner of the second cave. Count Cesare Spada – 25th April, 1498

'A month after I found the old piece of paper, I was arrested,' Faria said.

'Did you write the words on this second piece of paper?' asked Dantès.

'I did,' said Faria. 'I've thought and worked on these words for many years. If we escape together from here, half this treasure is yours. I give it to you. If I die here, and you escape alone, all the treasure is yours.'

'But the treasure belongs to you,' said Dantès. 'I'm not a member of your family.'

'I am a priest,' said Faria. 'Priests cannot marry and have children. You are like a son to me now, Edmond.'

11

Escape!

Time passed. Faria did not know the island of Monte Cristo, but Dantès had often sailed past it. He told Faria about it. Monte Cristo was near an island called Pianosa, which was between Corsica and Elba. They talked about places where the treasure might be hidden.

One night, Dantès woke up suddenly. Someone was calling him. He hurried through the tunnel to Faria's cell.

The old man was sitting on the floor and holding the side of his bed.

'My dear friend,' he whispered to Dantès. 'I am dying.'

'I saved you once,' said Dantès. 'I can save you again.'

'Well, you can try,' said Faria. 'But if I don't get better, pour *all* the medicine into my mouth this time.'

Dantès picked Faria up and put him on his bed. Then he went to the door of the cell to call for help.

'No!' said Faria. 'If the jailer finds you here, you'll never leave the prison. Go back to your own cell. If you *do* escape, go to Monte Cristo. Find the treasure!'

Dantès held the old man's hand.

'Goodbye – goodbye!' said Faria. 'Monte Cristo – don't forget Monte Cristo!'

The old man's head fell back and his mouth opened. Dantès quickly poured ten drops of the medicine into Faria's mouth. He waited. Ten minutes passed – then half an hour. Faria did not move. Dantès poured the rest of the medicine into Faria's mouth. The old man's body began to shake and he gave a short, sharp cry. He sat up in the bed and then fell back suddenly. He was dead.

Dantès stayed with Faria until the morning. When he heard the jailer coming with the breakfasts, he returned to his own cell. First, the jailer came with Dantès' breakfast. Then he went to Faria's cell. Dantès listened at the entrance to his tunnel. He heard the jailer go into Faria's cell. Then he heard him call for help.

'He's found Faria's body,' Dantès thought.

Other men ran to Faria's cell. Then soldiers arrived. Finally, the governor came to the old man's cell. Dantès listened.

'The priest is dead,' said the governor. 'Put him into a sack[61]. We'll remove him this evening at ten or eleven o'clock. Leave him now, and lock his cell.'

Dantès heard the men leave. After a moment, he crawled through the tunnel to Faria's cell. He saw the sack with Faria's body in it. Then he went and sat on the bed, next to his dear friend.

'If I could die, I would be with my old friend again,' he said. 'But I will *not* die now! I want to live and find happiness again. Perhaps I'll find Mercédès. There are people who betrayed me and I want revenge! But what shall I do? Only dead people leave Château d'If.'

As he said this, Dantès had an idea. First, he went to the fireplace and took Faria's tools and a knife from the hiding place. Next, he opened the sack and removed Faria's body. Then he took the body to his own cell, and put it on his bed. He covered Faria's body with a blanket and turned his head towards the wall.

'When the jailer brings my supper,' Dantès thought, 'he'll see Faria's body. But he won't see his face. He'll think that *I'm* sleeping on the bed.'

Dantès returned to Faria's cell quickly. He took Faria's needle and some thread[62]. Then he got inside the sack and sewed it up from the inside.

This was Dantès plan. After the jailers had buried him, Dantès would wait. When the jailers had left the graveyard, he would cut open the sack. He would push up the soft earth and escape. He hoped that he was strong enough to dig through the earth quickly. If he could not get to the air, he would die.

Dantès lay in the sack and waited. After many hours, he heard someone open the cell door. Two men picked up the sack and carried him out of the cell.

'He's a thin old man, but he's heavy,' said one jailer.

After a few minutes, Dantès felt the cold night air. They were outside the prison! The jailers put the sack down on the ground.

'Where am I?' thought Dantès. 'Is this the graveyard?'

'Lift the lamp,' said the first man. 'I can't see clearly. I can't find – ah, here it is!'

Dantès felt the jailers put something heavy next to the sack. Then they tied some rope around his feet.

'Have you tied the rope tightly to the stone?' asked the second man.

'Yes,' replied the first man.

Then they picked up the sack and walked about fifty

Then he got inside the sack and sewed it up from the inside.

metres. Dantès heard the sea crashing against rocks below the fortress.

'The weather is bad,' said the first man. 'It's not a nice night for a swim!'

The second man laughed. 'Well, he won't be trying to swim,' he said. 'One! Two! *Three!*'

At that moment, Dantès felt himself flying through the air. Then he was falling . . . falling. His body was pulled down by the heavy stone that was tied to his feet. SPLASH! He hit the ice-cold water. He gave a loud cry and the water closed over his head.

Dantès had been thrown into the sea. His grave was not in the earth. It was in the water. The *sea* was the graveyard of the Château d'If.

12

The Jeune-Amélie

Dantès had to get up to the surface of the water. He must have air. He cut open the sack, but the heavy stone pulled him down, deeper and deeper. Dantès pushed the knife down to his feet and cut the rope. Finally, the stone fell away and his feet were free. He kicked his legs. He must go up! He did not want to drown! He swam up until his head came out of the water. He took a big breath of air. Then he swam under the water again. He did not want the soldiers in the fortress to see him.

When his head came out of the water for the second time, Dantès was fifty metres from the rocky shore. He listened. He did not hear shouts from the prison. No one had seen him escape.

He began to swim away from the island. Soon, he could no longer see the fortress.

The sky became lighter. In a few hours the sun would rise. Rain began to fall and a cold wind began to blow. Dantès swam for another hour. Suddenly the sky became darker. At the same moment, he felt a sharp pain in his knee. He put his hand down and felt sharp rocks. He had reached the shore of an island.

'This must be Tiboulen,' thought Dantès. He knew that this small island was only a few kilometres from Chateau d'If. He pulled himself out of the water and walked a few metres onto the shore. Then he lay down and slept.

After an hour, Dantès was woken by the sound of thunder. There was a terrible storm above him. Lightning flashed, the wind blew, and rain fell heavily. Dantès opened his mouth and drank the rain-water. It was delicious.

He turned towards the sea and looked at the sky and the waves. There was another flash of lightning – and Dantès saw a fishing boat. It was close to the island. Suddenly, a huge wave threw the boat against the rocks of the shore. There was a loud crash and the wooden boat began to break. Dantès ran down to the rocks. The men in the boat fell into the sea. They saw Dantès and shouted, but he could not help them. All the men drowned.

At last, the wind stopped blowing and the sea became calm. When the sun rose, Dantès saw pieces of the fishing boat and a red fisherman's hat in the water. He looked towards Château d'If.

'In two or three hours, the jailer will find poor Faria's body in my cell,' he thought. 'Then everyone in the fortress will begin to search for me. They'll search the sea around If. And they'll tell the police in Marseille about my escape.'

A few minutes later, Dantès saw the sails of a ship. He watched it come towards Tiboulen. Suddenly, Dantès had an idea. He jumped into the sea, lifted the red hat out of the water, and put it on his head. Then he held a large piece of wood that had come from the fishing boat. He began to swim towards the sailing ship. When he was near the ship, Dantès took off the red hat and lifted it up in the air.

'Help! Help!' he shouted.

The sailors on the ship saw the red hat in Dantès' hand and they heard his shouts. Two sailors got into a small boat, lowered it from the ship, and began to row towards him.

Dantès began to swim towards the small boat, but he was very tired. He could not swim any further. His head went under the surface of the water. He was going to drown. Suddenly he felt someone put their hands under his arms. A few seconds later, the sailors had pulled him up out of the sea. Dantès lay in the bottom of the boat. His head fell back, his eyes closed and he heard nothing more. He had fainted.

When he opened his eyes again, Dantès was aboard the ship. It was sailing away from the Château d'If. Someone poured some rum into his mouth and the strong drink made him feel better.

A dark, heavy man came to speak to Dantès.

'You're on the ship, *Jeune-Amélie*,' he said. 'I am Captain Baldi. Who are you?'

Dantès did not want to tell the captain his name, or where he had come from. 'I–I'm a sailor,' he answered. He spoke in Italian. 'My home is on Malta. I–I was on a ship that sank in a storm last night. I was lucky. I fell into the sea and held onto a piece of wood. The captain of my ship and the rest of the crew drowned. Thank you for saving me.'

'Look! What's happening at the Château d'If?' said one of the sailors. He was pointing to the north.

Dantès looked up. He saw a small white cloud above the château. A few seconds later, he heard a loud explosion.

'A prisoner has escaped from the Château d'If,' said

'You're on the ship, Jeune-Amélie,' he said. 'I am Captain
Baldi. Who are you?'

Dantès. 'The soldiers are firing the fortress's cannon.'

The captain looked quickly at Dantès. Dantès was very thin and his face was pale. His hair and his beard were long and all his clothes were old and torn.

'Perhaps this man escaped from the prison,' thought Baldi. 'I don't care. If he's a good sailor, he'll be useful to us.'

'Maltese,' he said to Dantès, 'do you know the Mediterranean well? Do you know the best places to anchor a ship?'

'Yes,' Dantès replied. 'I've been sailing on this sea since I was a young boy.'

The captain turned to one of the crew. 'Jacopo,' he said. 'Give this man a shirt and a pair of trousers.'

Jacopo went away and came back with one of his own shirts and a pair of trousers. He gave them to Dantès.

'Thank you,' said Dantès. 'What is the date?'

Jacopo was surprised. 'Why do you ask me this? Have you forgotten?'

'I–I hurt my head when my ship sank,' said Dantès. 'I can't remember very much at all.'

'It's 28th February, 1829,' said Jacopo. 'Come with me, Maltese. I'll get you some food.'

Fourteen years had passed since Dantès had been arrested and taken to the Château d'If. He was now thirty-three years old.

13

The Treasure

The crew of the *Jeune-Amélie* were smugglers. At first, Captain Baldi suspected that Dantès was a customs officer. But very soon, Baldi was happy with 'the Maltese'. Everyone on the *Jeune-Amélie* liked Dantès, and Jacopo the Corsican, became his good friend. The captain saw that Dantès was a good sailor. He found out that Dantès knew many small islands where the smugglers could hide their ship. After this, Baldi asked no more questions and he paid Dantès well.

For two months, the *Jeune-Amélie* sailed along the coasts of the countries around the Mediterranean. At last, they reached Leghorn, in Italy.

Dantès went ashore to find a barber[63]. He asked the man to cut his long hair and shave his beard. When the barber had removed all of Dantès' beard with a sharp razor, Dantès looked in a mirror. He was surprised when he saw his face. He was thin and there were many more lines around his sad eyes.

'My family and friends won't recognize me,' he thought. 'I don't recognize myself.'

Next he bought new clothes – a pair of white trousers, a shirt with blue and white stripes, and a hat.

A few days later, the *Jeune-Amélie* left Leghorn and sailed south. The ship was carrying a cargo of cigars, sherry and wine. The smugglers were going to take these things to a secret place on the coast of Corsica. Another ship was going to smuggle the cargo to France.

The next morning, Captain Baldi saw Dantès standing on the deck of the *Jeune-Amélie*. The ship was passing the small island of Monte Cristo. Dantès was staring across the sea at the island. Every night for three months, Dantès had dreamed about the treasure on Monte Cristo.

'I could jump off the ship and swim to Monte Cristo in half an hour,' he thought. 'But what would the crew say? What would Captain Baldi think? The smugglers suspect that I have a secret. I don't want them to follow me. No, I must wait. I'll return to the island alone.'

Dantès had waited fourteen years for his freedom and now he was free. He could wait another six months or a year for his treasure. But was there *really* any treasure? Or was it only poor Faria's dream? Of course, there *was* Spada's letter. Dantès remembered every word of it.

———

Two months passed and the *Jeune-Amélie* returned to Leghorn. One evening, Captain Baldi took Dantès to an inn in the town. Dantès had visited the inn many years before. He knew that smugglers went there.

Baldi thought that Dantès would soon leave the *Jeune-Amélie*. But he wanted Dantès to stay and become a smuggler. He told Dantès his plan. The *Jeune-Amélie* was going to meet a Turkish ship which carried a cargo of Turkish carpets and cloth from Kashmir.

The two captains needed a secret place to meet. They were going to move the cargo from the Turkish ship to the *Jeune-Amélie*. The smugglers did not want the customs officers to see this.

'We'll use the island of Monte Cristo,' said Baldi to the Turkish captain. 'No customs officers will find us there. Take your cargo to the island and we'll collect it later.'

Dantès was very excited. This was his lucky chance! Now he could get to the island and find Faria's treasure.

Several days later, the *Jeune-Amélie* reached Monte Cristo. At ten o'clock that night, the crew dropped the ship's anchor and the *Jeune-Amélie* stopped near the shore. Dantès lowered a boat over the side of the ship and rowed towards the island.

The *Jeune-Amélie's* crew worked all through the night. They picked up the cargo which had been left by the Turkish smugglers. Then they loaded it onto the *Jeune-Amélie*. In the morning, everyone rested on the soft sand of the shore. But Dantès did not rest. He told the smugglers that he was going to shoot one of the wild goats that lived on the island.

'We'll have a good meal of goat meat when I return,' he said. Then he took a gun and walked away from the shore.

Jacopo called out, 'I'll come with you.'

Half an hour later, Dantès killed a small goat.

'Take it back to the others,' he told Jacopo. 'They can cook it. When the meat is cooked, fire a gun and I'll return.'

Jacopo went back to the shore with the goat and Dantès walked further across the island. He climbed up to the top of a high rock and looked down at the shore. The smugglers were busy by the fire.

Dantès remembered Count Spada's letter and the words that Faria had written. *Go ashore where there is a little creek. Walk east until you see a line of rocks. Lift the twentieth rock and find the entrance of two caves. The treasure is in the corner of the second cave.*

Dantès began to walk across the island. After more than an hour, he found a path between two walls of rock. He went down the path and onto the shore. As he walked beside the sea, Dantès looked at the rocks above the shore. He began to count them. One, two, three … Each rock had small marks on them. Had a man made these marks? But the twentieth rock had no marks on it.

'Perhaps I've made a mistake,' Dantès thought. 'There is no cave here, only a very large rock. Perhaps I'm going in the wrong direction. I'll go back and start again.'

He walked back past the rocks and along the path. When the smugglers saw Dantès, the captain called to him.

'Maltese!' he shouted. 'The meat is cooked!'

The men watched Dantès coming down to the shore. They saw him jumping from rock to rock. Suddenly, his foot slipped on the edge of a rock, and he fell.

The men ran to help him. When they reached Dantès, he was lying on the ground. They tried to lift him, but Dantès cried out.

'Stop!' he shouted. 'I've injured my back! I can't move. Leave me! Go and eat your meal. Let me rest.'

Later, the smugglers tried to move Dantès again. Once more, he cried out. His face was pale.

'Perhaps you've broken some of your ribs,' said Baldi. 'We'll stay here until this evening. We can try to move you then.'

'No, you must return to the *Jeune-Amélie*,' said Dantès. 'You must sell the cargo. Continue your journey. Leave me some bread and rum. And leave me some gunpowder[64] for my gun, and a pickaxe. I'll get better soon, I'm sure. Make a small fire for me here. I can shoot a goat and cook the meat on the fire. And I can use the pickaxe to build a shelter.'

'Very well,' said the captain. 'We'll be away for a week. We'll come back for you in seven days.'

Jacopo wanted to stay with Dantès.

'You're a good friend to me, Jacopo,' said Dantès. 'But you must go with the others.'

'Very well, Maltese,' said the Corsican. 'Good luck.'

An hour later, the *Jeune-Amélie* sailed away from Monte Cristo. When he could not see the ship's sails, Dantès stood up. There was nothing wrong with him. He had no injuries. He smiled, picked up the gun and the pickaxe, and ran towards the big rock. When he reached it, he walked all around it.

'How did Spada lift this rock without any help?' he said to himself. 'Of course! He didn't *lift* it, he *pushed it down* here!'

Dantès looked at the ground around the rock. Then he used his pickaxe to dig a small hole beside the rock. Next, he poured some gunpowder into the hole. He tore off a long piece of cloth from his shirt and put one end of it into the gunpowder. He made a flame and held it against the cloth. The piece of material began to burn. Dantès ran from the big rock and stood behind a smaller one. After a few seconds, the flame reached the gunpowder. It exploded with a loud bang.

Dantès saw that the big rock had moved a few metres. It was now lying on some soft earth and small stones at the edge of a slope. Dantès pushed against the rock with all his strength. After a moment or two, the rock moved and began to roll down the slope. The rock rolled faster and faster until it fell into the sea.

There was a flat, square stone where the rock had been lying. In the stone, there was a large metal ring. Dantès pulled on the ring and slowly lifted up the stone. It was a door! Below the door, there were some steps that went down under the ground. He had found the caves!

Dantès went down the steps into the first cave. The air in the cave was cool and pleasant, and daylight came through a hole in the roof. He looked round the cave, but it was empty. Then he remembered the words in the letter: *The treasure is in the corner of the second cave.* Where was the second cave?

He knocked on the walls of the cave with the pickaxe. In one place, the sound was different. Dantès hit the wall again. But this time, he used the sharp end of the pickaxe. He hit the wall hard and the rock fell away. Behind it, there were some square white stones. Dantès removed these quickly and soon there was a big hole. When he climbed through the hole to the second cave, he saw that it was empty.

'Perhaps the treasure is buried in the corner, under the floor,' he thought.

He walked across to the corner of the cave, and began to dig. After a few minutes, he had removed many metres of earth and stones. Suddenly, his pickaxe hit something. He dug deeper. It was a wooden chest! Dantès dug the earth away until he could see all of the chest. On the top of it, there was a square of silver with a picture of a sword. Faria had told Dantès that this was the mark of the Spadas.

Dantès opened the lid of the chest with the pickaxe. Inside, there was a wonderful treasure – gold coins, silver and very many jewels of all kinds! Dantès touched some of the coins and the jewels. Was he awake, or was it a dream?

Inside the chest, there was a wonderful treasure.

He laughed and danced round the cave. Then he fell onto his knees and thanked God.

The next day, Dantès began to think more calmly. He filled his pockets with coins and jewels. Then he put the chest back into the hole in the floor. He covered the hole with some earth and stones and walked back through the caves. He shut the stone door at the top of the steps. Then he covered the door with earth and stones and he planted some small bushes in the earth. Next, he took a branch from a tree and carefully removed all his footmarks.

———

Six days later, the *Jeune-Amélie* returned to Monte Cristo. Jacopo and three other men rowed a longboat to the shore. Dantès told the smugglers that he felt much better.

When the *Jeune-Amélie* reached Leghorn, Dantès went to a jeweller's shop. He sold four of the smallest jewels from the treasure chest. The jeweller gave Dantès twenty thousand francs for the jewels and he asked no questions.

The next day, Dantès bought a boat and went to speak to Jacopo. Dantès and Jacopo had become good friends. Dantès liked the Corsican and he needed his help. But he did not tell the smuggler about the treasure. He gave the boat to Jacopo and asked him to sail it to Marseille. Then he gave Jacopo some gold coins.

'Take this money to pay a crew,' he said. Jacopo was very surprised.

'My uncle has died and left me a lot of money,' said Dantès. 'I won't have to work as a sailor any more.'

Then he told Jacopo that he knew how to get a lot more money. Jacopo was interested in this idea. He agreed to sail the boat to Marseille.

'When you reach Marseille,' said Dantès, 'find out everything about an old man called Louis Dantès, and a young woman called Mercédès.'

Dantès went to Captain Baldi and told him that he was leaving the *Jeune-Amélie*. He gave presents to the captain and the crew and said goodbye. Then he went to buy a yacht. This little boat was small and fast, and Dantès could sail it alone.

Dantès sailed first to Genoa, and then to the island of Monte Cristo. When he reached Monte Cristo, Dantès went ashore and walked all around the island. There was no one there. He was alone. That night, he slept for only a few hours. He was very excited.

At sunrise, Dantès began to remove the treasure. He worked all through the day. By the evening, all the treasure was hidden in his yacht.

For seven days, Dantès watched the sea. He sailed slowly around the island. On the eighth day, he saw the sails of Jacopo's boat. Soon, he was anchored beside it.

Jacopo told him the sad news that he had heard in Marseille. Old Louis Dantès was dead, and Mercédès had disappeared.

_____

On a fine day, a few weeks later, Dantès arrived in the port of Marseille.

'I can't use the name Edmond Dantès any more,' he thought. 'People will be looking for Edmond Dantès – the prisoner who escaped from Château d'If. I want to stay a free man. A lucky chance and dear Faria have made me a rich man. Perhaps I can start a new life with a new name. I shall become, "The Count of Monte Cristo!"' He smiled. 'I like it,' he said.

Now it was time to find his enemies and take revenge.

Points for Understanding

1

1 What are these things: *mast, a port, starboard, anchor, deck, sail, oars, cabin, cargo?*
2 Who are these people and how are they connected to the *Pharaon:* Edmond Dantès, Danglars, Leclère, Mercédès, Morrel?

2

Good and bad news is given in this chapter. (a) What is the news? (b) Who tells it? (c) Who hears it?

3

Why has Dantès been arrested? What is he accused of?

4

Which things in this chapter might improve or ruin Villefort's career? Give reasons.

5

How does Dantès try to buy his freedom? What happens next?

6

Duc de Blacas, Dandré, Villefort, Marshall Bertrand and General Quesnel. Have these people served their employers well or badly? Give reasons.

7

1 Who comes to the hotel in Paris? Why?
2 Who went to 53, Rue Saint-Jacques? Why?
3 Who is coming to Lyons on 10th or 12th March? Why?

8

How does Villefort trick Morrel?

9

How does Prisoner Number 34 meet Prisoner Number 27?

10

1 Why is Faria in Château d'If ?
2 What does he tell Dantès? Why does he tell him this?

11

How does Dantès escape from the fortress?

12

What does Dantès tell the men on *Jeune-Amélie* when they pull him from the sea? Do you think that they believe his story? Why? Why not?

13

1 Why are these things important in this chapter? (a) the goat (b) the twentieth rock (c) the gunpowder (d) the yacht.
2 How do you think that Dantès will take his revenge?

Glossary

1 **innkeeper** (page 4)
an *inn* is a place where travellers can rest or eat a meal. The owner of the inn is an *innkeeper*.

2 **secretary** (page 4)
Dumas arranged meetings, wrote letters and prepared documents for the duke.

3 **debts** (page 4)
debts are amounts of money that you owe. If you cannot repay the money, you are *in debt*. The people to whom you owe money are *creditors*.

4 **love affair** (page 4)
a sexual relationship. Two people who love each other very much are *lovers*. The word is also used for two people who have a sexual relationship.

5 **XVI** (page 5)
Roman numbers which are the symbols for the number 'sixteen'. X = 10, V = 5, I = 1. Louis XVI was the 'sixteenth' king of France with the name Louis.

6 **rule** (page 5)
officially control a country or an area. A person who officially controls a country or an area is a *ruler*.

7 **trial** (page 5)
a person who breaks a law is *arrested* by the police. The police take the person to a police station and ask questions. If the police find out that the person did break a law, they *accuse* the person of *commiting a crime*. The person is taken to a law court and officials of the court (lawyers and the judge) ask the person questions. This is a *trial*. When all the information is given correctly and the court decides carefully, this is a *fair trail*. If a court decides that the person did commit the crime, the person is *guilty*. The person is a *criminal*. If a court decides that the person did not commit the crime, the person is *innocent*.

8 **treason** – *accuse someone of treason* (page 5)
someone who has done something which makes trouble for their own country is a *traitor*. A traitor's crime is called *treason*. If someone tells another person that they are a traitor, they are *accusing that person of treason*.

9 **executed** – *to be executed* (page 5)
   be killed because you have broken an important law.
10 **career** (page 6)
   a job that you are trained to do. If you want your *career* to be more
   successful, you want to *improve your career*. If your job is harmed or
   ends because you have done something wrong, your *career is ruined*.
11 **supporters** (page 6)
   people who help someone because they believe that person's ideas.
   They *support* that person.
12 **employed** – *to employ* (page 6)
   pay someone to work for you. You are that person's *employer*.
13 **special police agents** (page 6)
   police officers who do secret work.
14 **abdicated** – *to abdicate* (page 6)
   if a ruler *abdicates*, he or she gives up their power to rule a country.
15 **cargomaster** (page 8)
   the goods that a ship carries are called *cargo*. The *cargomaster* looks
   after the cargo. He makes sure that the cargo is *loaded* onto the ship
   correctly. And he gives orders for the cargo to be *unloaded*.
16 **prosecutor** (page 8)
   an important French official in the nineteenth century. *Prosecutors*
   asked criminals questions and sometimes sent them to prison.
17 **adviser** (page 8)
   a person who helps someone decide what to do.
18 **port** (page 11)
   an area of water near a city, where ships stop. There are buildings
   around a *port*. A *harbour* is a smaller place where small ships stop. A
   quay is the hard ground beside the water in a port or a harbour.
   Cargo, or passengers, are moved on or off ships from a quay. NOTE:
   Port is also the word for the left side of a ship. *Starboard* is the
   right side of a ship. (See the picture on page 9.)
19 **rowed** – *to row* (page 11)
   pull a small boat through the water using two long poles called *oars*.
   The oars are attached to the sides of the boat.
20 **brain-fever** (page 12)
   an illness of the brain.
21 **buried him at se**a – *to bury someone at sea* (page 12)
   when someone dies, their body is *buried*. It is usually put into the
   ground in a place called a *graveyard*. If a person dies when they are
   on a ship and it is far from land, their body is put into the water.
   The person is *buried at sea*.

84

22 **aboard** (page 12)

in or on a ship. If a person invites someone to '*come aboard*' he is inviting that person to come onto his ship. The *shore* is land which is on the edge of a lake, river, or the sea. When someone goes to the land from a ship, they are *going ashore*.

23 **angry expression** (page 12)

the way that a person's face shows their feelings is their *expression*. Your expression shows if you are happy, sad, angry, in love, worried, etc.

24 **honest** (page 12)

an *honest* person tells the truth and does not steal things.

25 **confident** (page 12)

not feel nervous or frightened.

26 **customs officers** (page 13)

government officials who make sure that *tax* (extra money) is paid for goods that are brought into a country. Anyone who brings goods into a country and does not pay tax is a *smuggler*.

27 **Les Catalans** (page 15)

the village had this name because the people who lived there had come from Catalonia, a north-eastern region of Spain.

28 **tailor** (page 17)

a person who makes and repairs clothes.

29 **admirers** (page 17)

people who like the way that someone looks, works, or behaves.

30 **suspect** (page 22)

if you think that something is wrong, but you are not sure, you are *suspicious*. You *suspect* a person of doing something wrong. That person is a *suspect*. If you think that something is strange, you might look at it *suspiciously*. If a thing seems strange to you, and you are worried about it, that thing can be described as *suspicious*. But if you say, 'That woman is suspicious', you mean 'She suspects somebody or something'. You do not mean 'I suspect her'. Your worries about something or someone are called *suspicions*. NOTE: The verb is pronounced sus**pect**. The adverb is pronounced sus**pic**iously. The noun is pronounced **sus**pect.

31 **proof** (page 23)

things that show how someone did something wrong.

32 **jealous** (page 28)

if someone has something that you want, or does something that you want to do, you are *jealous*. *Jealousy* is this feeling of sadness and anger.

33 **betrayed** – *to betray* (page 28)
do or say something that harms someone, or makes danger for them.

34 **drink to the health of someone** (page 28)
wish someone well and then drink some wine.

35 **strong political opinions** (page 30)
strong thoughts about how rulers or governments should do their work.

36 **respect** – *to have respect* (page 30)
like someone and think that they do their work well.

37 **recognize** (page 30)
know something or someone and remember where you have seen it, or them, before.

38 **Smyrna** (page 30)
the old name for Izmir in Turkey.

39 **make me a promise** – *to make a promise* (page 31)
say very strongly that you will do something when someone asks you.

40 **fortress** (page 31)
a strong building with walls that are made of stone.

41 **courtyard** (page 35)
a place with walls, or other buildings, around it.

42 **jailers** (page 35)
people who work in prisons and guard the prisoners.

43 **governor** (page 35)
the chief official in a prison.

44 **dungeon** (page 36)
a dark room that is under the ground beneath a castle.

45 **provinces** (page 37)
parts of a country.

46 **trust** (page 37)
believe that someone is truthful, kind and helpful.

47 **plot** (page 37)
someone who has made a *plot against you*, has a plan to harm you.

48 **serve** (page 38)
work for an employer, or your country.

49 **ambitious** (page 39)
someone who wants to be successful, rich, or famous is *ambitious*.

50 **bowing** – *to bow* (page 39)
bend your head and the top part of your body towards someone.

51 **loyal** (page 42)

a *loyal* person wants to work, or help their friends, even in difficult times.

52 **side-whiskers** (page 43)

long hair that men grow on the sides of their faces. *Side-whiskers* were a popular fashion for men at this time.

53 **medal** (page 43)

a prize which is given to a person who has done something brave or good. Medals can be made from gold, silver, or bronze metal.

54 **razor** (page 46)

a kind of very sharp knife. Razors are used to *shave* – completely remove the hair – which grows on men's faces.

55 **tunnel** (page 50)

a passage under the ground.

56 **inspector of prisons** (page 50)

a person who checks prisons and the prisoners in them.

57 **cement** (page 53)

grey powder that is mixed with water. Bricks or stones in a wall are fixed together with *cement.*

58 **failed** – *to fail* (page 56)

not succeed.

59 **lucky chance** (page 58)

a time when you have good luck.

60 **revenge** – *to take revenge on someone* (page 60)

do something bad to someone because they have hurt you, or made you very unhappy.

61 **sack** (page 65)

a large bag made from rough material.

62 **needle and some thread** (page 66)

a *needle* is small, very thin tool which is used to join two pieces of cloth together. There is a hole at one end, and a sharp point at the other end. A *thread* – a very long, very thin cord is pulled through the two pieces of cloth with a needle. When you do this, you are *sewing up* the two pieces of cloth.

63 **barber** (page 73)

a person who is paid to cut men's hair or shave their faces.

64 **gunpowder** (page 76)

a black powder that makes an explosion when it burns.

Dictionary extracts adapted from the Macmillan English Dictionary © Bloomsbury Publishing PLC 2002 and © A & C Black Publishers Ltd 2005

Vocabulary: meanings of words from the story

Put the words and phrases in the box next to the correct meanings.

revenge   trial   arrest   cargo   governor   starboard
fiancée   experience   confident   loyal   quay
anchor   admire   customs   expression   ambitious
dungeon   tunnel   debt   accuse   prosecutor
treason   innocent   trust   tailor

1		things that are being sent by ship, plane, train, or truck
2		knowledge and skill gained through time spent in a job or activity
3		a feeling of being able to do something well – so you are not nervous or worried
4		a heavy object that is dropped into the sea to stop a ship moving
5		a government department that collects taxes on goods that people bring into a country
6		an amount of money that you owe to someone
7		to have feelings of great respect for someone or something
8		a lawyer whose job is to prove that a person accused of a crime is guilty; in the story he is an important official in Marseilles
9		the crime of helping your country's enemies to destroy your country's government
10		not guilty of a crime
11		to take a person to a police station because the person is believed to have committed a crime
12		the process of examining a criminal case in a court of law

13		to say that someone has done something wrong or has committed a crime
14		the chief official of a prison
15		a dark, underground room in a castle or prison
16		a feeling of confidence in someone who you believe to be honest, fair and reliable
17		determined to be successful, rich, famous, etc.
18		faithful – a feeling of duty and love that makes you support someone or something
19		an underground passage
20		something that you do to hurt someone because they have hurt you
21		a hard surface next to the sea or river where boats can stop
22		the right-hand side of a ship
23		the woman to whom a man is engaged; the woman a particular man will marry
24		a person whose job is to make clothes
25		the look on someone's face that shows what their thoughts or feelings are

Writing: rewrite sentences

Rewrite the sentences using the words and phrases in the previous exercise to replace the underlined words.

> **Example:** The captain dropped <u>a heavy object in the water to stop the ship.</u>
>
> You write: The captain *dropped anchor to stop the ship.*

1 Did you say that the <u>goods you are carrying on the ship</u> are safe?
   Did you say

2 His father repaid <u>the money that he owed</u> to Caderousse.
   His father

3 Danglars thought that Dantès did not have enough <u>knowledge and skill</u> to be captain.
   Danglars

4 He was <u>not nervous or worried</u>.
   He was

5 <u>The government tax officials</u> are about to come onboard.

6 Many men <u>look at</u> Mercédès and want to marry her.
   Many men

7 Danglars wrote a letter to the <u>important official</u> in Marseilles.
   Danglars

8 'Edmond Dantès, I have come to <u>take you to the police station</u>,' said the officer.
   'Edmond Dantès,

9 Dantès is accused of <u>helping the enemies of the government</u>.
   Dantès

10 I am sure that Dantès is <u>not guilty</u>.
   I am

11 He was not <u>taken to a court of law and allowed to speak</u>.
   He was

12 The <u>chief official</u> of the prison is asleep.
   The

13 I <u>believe</u> in this man.
   I

14 Villefort is <u>determined to be successful</u>.
   Villefort

15 Quesnel was not <u>faithful</u> to Napoleon.
   Quesnel

16 A prisoner was digging a <u>passage under the ground</u>.
   A prisoner

17 Dantès wanted to escape and <u>hurt the people who were his enemies</u>.
   Dantès

18 'Mercédès isn't my lover – she is <u>the woman I'm going to marry</u>,' said Dantès.

19 Caderousse <u>made and repaired clothes</u>.

20 Morrel stood on the <u>side of the harbour</u> where the boat was about to dock.

Vocabulary: anagrams

The letters of each word are mixed up. Write the words correctly.
The first one is an example.

Example:	GENEVER *revenge*	something bad which you want to do to a person who has hurt you
1	SFORTERS	a strong, well-protected building that is used for defence or as a prison
2	NANCON	a large and powerful gun, used in the past to shoot metal balls
3	ROBURAH	an area of water near the land where it is safe for boats to stay
4	EXIPACK	a tool used for breaking roads and other hard surfaces
5	LEGLINETINT	good at thinking clearly and quickly
6	SONETH	does not tell lies and cheat people
7	GOYAVE	a long trip, especially by boat or in space
8	INCHA	a series of metal rings connected to each other, used for fastening, pulling and lifting things
9	REPROME	a man who rules an empire
10	GRAMARIE	the relationship between two people who are husband and wife; also a wedding celebration
11	SINDAL	a piece of land that is completely surrounded by water

12	ROTIRAT	someone who is not loyal to his own country or government and helps his country's enemies
13	CUPESTS	someone who the police believe may have committed a crime
14	RERACE	a job or series of jobs, especially professional positions, which you spend most of your life doing
15	URNI	to destroy something
16	RAJILE	someone whose job is to guard people in prison
17	PUSTROP	to help a person or organization to be successful; to uphold an idea
18	PRENTMATED	a section in a government, organization, or business that deals with one type of work
19	GARREICA	a vehicle with wheels that is pulled by horses and carries people
20	CUTEXEE	to kill someone as a punishment for a crime

Grammar: syntax

Put the words into the correct order to make sentences.

> **Example:** Dantès each few hours only saw daylight for a day.
> You write: *Dantès only saw daylight for a few hours each day.*

1 In an old fireplace of the corner there was one priest's cell.

_____

2 Dantès promised that he would teach Faria everything he that knew.

_____

3 The special ink were written in words, and the fire from the heat made the words appear!

_____

4 They might be hidden places where about the treasure talked.

_____

5 Dantès heard the rocks crashing against the fortress below sea.

_____

6 Someone made some him better rum and his feel mouth poured the drink into strong.

_____

7 Lift two the rock entrance and find the twentieth of caves.

_____

8 Faria made dear me A lucky man and have a rich chance.

_____

Vocabulary Choice: words which are related in meaning

Which word is most closely related? Look at the example and circle the word which is most closely related to the word in bold.

	Example:				
	popular	national	(liked)	tree	company

1	**royal**	money	real	regal	faithful
2	**harm**	leg	uphold	body	hurt
3	**military**	civilian	army	ships	trade
4	**rule**	marker	board	plate	govern
5	**power**	authority	cannon	fortress	prison
6	**harbour**	key	starboard	port	train
7	**fever**	noise	calm	owner	illness
8	**order**	serial	dirt	flower	command
9	**voyage**	journey	carriage	vehicle	wagon
10	**packet**	book	papers	cup	soup

Vocabulary: opposite meanings

Look at the example and circle the word which is nearest to the opposite meaning of the word in bold.

	Example:				
	leave	go	exit	quit	(stay)

1	**honest**	cheat	warm	true	faithful
2	**angry**	mad	annoyed	hot	calm
3	**rich**	wealthy	prosperous	heavy	poor
4	**polite**	civil	respectful	admired	rude
5	**enemy**	rival	friend	foe	ally
6	**drunk**	full	empty	sober	bottle
7	**proud**	arrogant	rude	high	modest
8	**special**	particular	ordinary	distinctive	unique

Published by Macmillan Heinemann ELT
Between Towns Road, Oxford OX4 3PP
Macmillan Heinemann ELT is an imprint of
Macmillan Publishers Limited
Companies and representatives throughout the world

Heinemann is a registered trademark of Harcourt Education, used under licence.

EAN 978–1–4050–8419–2

This version of *The Treasure of Monte Cristo* by Alexandre Dumas was
retold by John Escott for Macmillan Readers
First published 2007
Text © Macmillan Publishers Limited 2007
Design and illustration © Macmillan Publishers Limited 2007
This version first published 2007

Illustrations by Mike Lacey and Martin Sanders
Cover photograph by Gary Leighty/Stock Connection Blue/Alamy

Printed and bound in Thailand
2011 2010 2009 2008 2007

10 9 8 7 6 5 4 3 2 1